MW01671484

THE *Rider* BOOK OF LISTS

100 lists honouring 100 years of the Saskatchewan Roughriders

Rod Nasewich

Sheldon Green

First printed in 2010

Contact: riderbookoflists@hotmail.com

Published by the authors. Regina, Saskatchewan, Canada

Library and Archives Canada Cataloguing in Publication

Nasewich, Rod, 1963-
The Rider book of lists : 100 lists honouring 100 years of the Saskatchewan Roughriders / Rod Nasewich, Sheldon Green.

Includes bibliographical references.
ISBN 978-0-9866828-0-3

1. Saskatchewan Roughriders (Football team)--History.
2. Saskatchewan Roughriders (Football team)--Miscellanea.
I. Green, Sheldon R. (Sheldon Robert), 1963- II. Title.

GV948.3.S37N38 2010 796.335'6409712445 C2010-904861-X

Table of Contents

Introduction

The idea for a Rider Book of Lists originated during the team's thrilling 2009 Grey Cup run, as our way of honouring the Riders' 100th anniversary in 2010.

While the idea for the book may have started in late 2009, our affinity for the team is as the result of over 40 years of watching, hearing about, and cheering for the Riders - having both been born and raised in Saskatchewan. Even though our respective education and career paths took us outside the province for a time and back again, our fascination with the Riders and their exploits has never diminished – not unlike most Rider fans.

This book takes a different look at the Riders, as players and individuals, as a team and organization, and even as a culture. It is meant to contribute in a unique way to the team's history, its legends and lore, and complement the considerable material on the Saskatchewan Roughriders, whether published or otherwise in the public domain. Most of all, it hopes to appeal to all generations of Rider fans.

Where our lists have data that may well be found elsewhere, such as award and trophy winners, and all-time leaders and record holder lists, we tried to provide additional information and context of value for both the casual fan and the statistical enthusiast.

Our lists are not meant to be definitive or exhaustive, but we do think they are accurate, engaging and entertaining. We have tried to cover areas and topics other books on the Riders have not, and in so doing span the depth, breadth and reach of the team and its 100 years of history.

We hope you enjoy reading our lists as much as we enjoyed developing and compiling them. Any errors or omissions are entirely unintentional, and we welcome and encourage readers to contact us and let us know of any additions we could include in future editions. You can contact us at: riderbookoflists@hotmail.com.

Acknowledgements

We would like to thank the following individuals for their personal assistance in helping us during the completion of this book: Doug Rogers, Steve Mazurak, Ted Urness, Erin Mclauchlan, Keith Comstock, Al Benecick, and Corey Mueller. Finally, we thank our families, Jennifer, Aiden, Addison, Susanne, Jake, and Carl for putting up with, and sharing in, our Rider pride.

A Note on Abbreviations:
For the benefit of football fans and our readers, we have included player and executive positions and years with the Riders whenever listing individuals. Where possible, we spelled out the positions; where space did not allow it, we used the following abbreviations, most of which are widely recognized, but some represent older terms no longer in use:

C – center; CB – cornerback; DB - defensive back; DE – defensive end;
DL – defensive lineman; DT - defensive tackle; E – end; FB – fullback;
FL - flanker (now called receiver); FW – flying wing (slotback);
G – guard; GM – general manager; HB – halfback; HC – head coach;
IW – inside wing (guard); K – kicker; KR – kick returner;
LB – linebacker; LS – long snapper; MW – middle wing (tackle);
OG – offensive guard; OL – offensive lineman; OT – offensive tackle;
OW – outside wing (end); P – punter; PK – placekicker;
QB – quarterback; RB – running back; S – safety; SB – slotback;
SE – split end (wide receiver); T – tackle; TE – tight end;
WR – wide receiver

I. On the Field

13 "Green" & "White" Riders

We know Rider fans bleed green, but here are thirteen players who embodied the Riders in name and on the field...

1. **Pete Green** – 1910
   Pete Green played one game as middle wing (tackle) in the Riders' inaugural 1910 season (as the Regina Rugby Club). The team lost all four of its games that year to Moose Jaw.

2. **Norman White** – 1912-13
   White played seven of eight regular season games in the team's 1912 and 1913 seasons as a flying wing (slotback) scoring one point.

3. **Nelson "Nellie" Greene** – 1950-53
   Nelson "Nellie" Greene played fullback and halfback for the Riders in the early 1950s after playing with the Ottawa Rough Riders for three seasons. His first season with the Riders (1950) was his best with the team, scoring four touchdowns.

4. **Reg Whitehouse** – 1952-66
   Whitehouse played for fifteen seasons as a guard, tackle and kicker, and is fourth all time among Riders in games played and tenth in points scored. His final game was the Grey Cup victory in 1966. He was inducted into the Rider Plaza of Honor in 1992.

5. **John Green** – 1953
   John Green was a defensive back for the Riders in 1953. Before joining the Riders, he played five seasons for the Philadelphia Eagles (1947-1951) and before that, college football at Tulsa.

6. **Tom Whitehouse** – 1958-59
   Tom Whitehouse played guard for the Riders for a couple of seasons in the late 1950s.

7. **Marcellus Greene** – 1982
   Marcellus Greene came to the Riders from the Argonauts in a trade that saw quarterback Joe Barnes go to Toronto, breaking up the "JJ Barnagel" quarterback tandem (John Hufnagel stayed with the Riders). Greene was cut in 1983 and returned to the Argos.

8. **Richard White** – 1984-85
   Richard White, a graduate of Simon Fraser University, played linebacker for the Roughriders. He also played for the BC Lions in the early 1980s.

9. **Sammy Greene** – 1984
The Riders were one of about a dozen professional football stops for outspoken wide receiver Sammy Greene whose off field activities often overshadowed his on-field ones. Greene played five games with the Riders catching 20 passes for 300 yards and three touchdowns before being released mid-season.

10. **Andrew Greene** – 1997, 1999-06
All-star offensive tackle Andrew Greene spent most of his career with the Riders with a few stints in between in the NFL. When a Rider, he was a five-time Western All-Star, four time CFL all-star, and the league's Most Outstanding Offensive Lineman in 2003. Ironically, Greene was playing with the Bombers in 2007 when the Riders beat them winning their third Grey Cup. In 2009, after being released by the Argonauts, the Roughriders signed Greene so he could retire in Green and White as a Roughrider.

11. **George White** – 2000-02
White was a defensive back/linebacker and two-time western all-star, and the West's Most Outstanding Canadian in 2000. Andrew Greene was the West's Outstanding Offensive Lineman the same year, making "Greene & White" the western reps at the CFL awards.

12. **Chris White** – 2002-03
White was a defensive tackle and played in the injury-laden 2002 season, before being released in early 2003.

13. **Nealon Greene** – 2002-05
Nealon Greene came to the Riders after stints in Toronto and Edmonton, and during his time with the Riders became their leading rushing quarterback. He is among the top ten Rider QBs in passing attempts, completions, passing yardage and touchdowns. In 2006, Greene was traded to the Alouettes, and was released the following season

What's in a Name?
50 Great Rider Nicknames

1. **"Slabs"** Merrick – Inside Wing (Guard), 1910-13
2. Alf **"Tiny"** Styles – Inside/Outside/Wing, 1911-14, 1919-20
3. **"Doc"** Bean – Middle Wing (Tackle), 1943
4. **"Moose"** Stinson – Half Back, 1910-14
5. **"Punk"** Thompson – Outside Wing (End), 1913
6. N.J. **"Piffles"** Taylor – Quarterback, 1914-15, 1919
7. **"Smoke"** Robson – Fullback, 1919-20
8. **"Bricks"** Peebles – Half Back, 1921-27
9. Frank **"Hoot"** York – Middle Wing (Tackle), 1926, 1932
10. Eddie **"Dynamite"** James – Halfback (Running Back), 1928-29, 1931
11. **"Jersey"** Jack Campbell – Centre/Slotback, 1929-35
12. Fred **"Tubby"** Renwick – Centre/Outside Wing (End), 1931-36
13. R.E. **"Stonewall"** Jackson – Middle Wing/Halfback, 1930
14. Al Ritchie **"The Silver Fox"** – GM 1921-24, HC1930-32, 1935, 1942
15. Fred **"Ripper"** Ray – Half Back, 1936-37
16. Dean **"Bad Man"** Griffing – Centre/HC, 1936-41, 1943, GM 1954-57
17. Jack **"Tiny"** Thompson – Middle Wing (Tackle), 1931-39
18. Walter **"Oke"** Olson – Quarterback, 1934-35
19. Jim **"Pheasant"** Partridge – Outside Wing (End), 1934-39
20. Jim **"Buzz"** Faraset – Half Back, 1938
21. Joe **"Joker"** Milanov – Half Back, 1942, 1945
22. Bill **"Bus"** Orban – Half Back, 1941-42
23. Harry **"Harpo"** Stillwell – Snapback (Centre), 1940
24. Clarence **"Toar"** Springstein – Tackle, 1939-41, 1946, 1949-52
25. Harry **"Blackjack"** Smith – Head Coach, 1951

26. Ron Atchison **"Big Atch"** – Defensive Tackle, 1952-68

27. Bobby Marlow **"The Alabama Basher"** – Fullback/LB, 1953-60

28. Don **"Knobby"** Walsh – Defensive Tackle, 1955-64

29. Larry Isbell **"Laughing Larry"** – DB/Punter, 1954-58

30. Carlton Chester **"Cookie"** Gilchrist – Halfback/Fullback, 1958

31. Bill Baker **"The Undertaker"** – DE, 1968-73, 1977-78

32. Ron Lancaster **"The Little General"** – Quarterback, 1963-78

33. Hugh Campbell **"Gluey Hughy"** – Flanker (Receiver), 1963-67, 1969

34. Wayne **"Clamps"** Shaw – Linebacker, 1961-72

35. **"The Slot Machines"** – Ray Elgaard & Jeff Fairholm – Slotbacks, 1988-93 (playing together those years)

36. Sylvester **"Molly"** McGee – Running Back, 1976-79

37. Anthony **"Stony"** Parker – Defensive Tackle, 1979

38. **"JJ Barnagel"** – John Hufnagel & Joe Barnes – Quarterbacks, 1980-81 (playing together those years)

39. Joe **"Papa Joe"** Faragalli – Head Coach, 1981-83

40. Joe **"747"** Adams – Quarterback, 1982-83

41. Alfred **"Jitter"** Fields – Linebacker, 1985

42. Joe Paopao **"The Throwin' Samoan"** – Quarterback, 1984-86

43. Donald **"Narco"** Narcisse – Receiver, 1987-99

44. Bob **"Polecat"** Poley – Centre/Tackle/Guard, 1978-84, 1988-92

45. Mike **"Scooter"** McGruder – Cornerback, 1986-88

46. Tom **"The Bomb"** Burgess – Quarterback, 1987-89, 1994-95

47. Fred **"Air"** McNair – Quarterback, 1992 *(the original "Air McNair")*

48. Dave Ridgway **"Robokicker"** – Placekicker, 1982-95

49. Scott **"Pootch"** Hendrickson – Centre/Guard, 1992-97

50. Ventson Donelson **"The Hitman"** – Defensive Back, 1991-2000

Do you know of other great Rider nicknames? Pass them along; contact: riderbookoflists@hotmail.com

Offensive Overload!
8 High Scoring Games

Here are eight of the highest scoring games in Rider history, with total points scored by both teams of 90 or more...

1. **106 – October 28, 2000; Riders 54 at Edmonton 52 (OT)**
   Second highest in CFL history (the highest is 111, scored by Toronto & BC in 1990).
2. **105 – July 1, 2010: Riders 54 at home to Montreal 51 (OT)**
   Third highest in CFL history; the 2010 regular season home opener for the Riders, and a rematch of the 2009 Grey Cup.
3. **104 – July 28, 2000; Riders 52 at home to Calgary 52 (OT)**
   Fourth highest in CFL history and the highest tied game in CFL history.
4. **97 – August 21, 1991; Riders 47 at home to BC 50**
   The 1991 season was the Riders' highest in terms of points scored, both for (606) and against (710).
5. **96 – September 21, 1991; Riders 49 at BC 47**
   This game was exactly one month after #3, the third highest scoring game in Rider history.
6. **93 – October 23, 1993; Riders 48 at home to Calgary 45**
   The Riders went 11-7 in 1993 and lost the West Semi-Final to Edmonton.
7. **92 – August 17, 2003; Riders 51 at home to Ottawa 41**
   The Riders went 11-7 in 2003 (Winnipeg and BC both had identical records) and finished third in the West. They beat the Bombers in the West Semi-Final and lost the West Final to Edmonton. Ottawa (Renegades) went 7-11, finishing third in the East, but BC would crossover to the East Semi-Final with their 11-7 record, and lose to Toronto.
8. **90 – September 8, 1991; Riders 41 at Winnipeg 49 (OT)**
   This was the third high scoring game in a month in 1991 (along with #3 and #4 noted above); the Riders went 6-12 in 1991 finishing 4th and out of the playoffs.

Defense Rules!
9 Low Scoring Games

Here are nine of the lowest scoring games in Rider history, with total points scored by both teams of less than five...

1. **0 – October 26, 1929; Riders 0 at Saskatoon 0**
   The Riders finished first in 1929, and were West Champs but lost the Grey Cup to Hamilton.
2. **1 – August 18, 1948; Riders 0 at home to Toronto 1**
   This was an exhibition match, and the Riders would finish second with a 3-9 record and lose in the playoffs to Calgary.
3. **3 – September 13, 1930; Riders 3 at Saskatoon 0**
   The Riders went undefeated at 4-0 in the 1930 regular season.
4. **4 – October 13, 1923; Riders 1 at home to Saskatoon 3**
   This was the only Rider loss in the season, and the Riders would go on to their first Grey Cup game.
5. **4 – November 17, 1930; Riders 4 at Vancouver 0**
   This was the 1930 West Final. The Riders would go to the Grey Cup against Toronto Balmy Beach, losing 11-6.
6. **4 – September 3, 1932; Riders 0 at Winnipeg 4**
   This was a pre-season match. The Riders would go 5-1 that season and head to their fifth consecutive Grey Cup appearance.
7. **4 – September 14, 1935; Riders 0 at home to Sarnia 4**
   An exhibition match of the previous year's Grey Cup in which Sarnia won 20-12.
8. **4 – September 2, 1940; Riders 3 at home to Winnipeg 1**
   An early Labour Day Classic, Winnipeg officially became the Blue Bombers in 1936.
9. **4 – October 27, 1945; Riders 1 at home to Calgary 3**
   One of only two league games played in 1945 (both playoff games) due to World War II.

18 Top Rider Quarterbacks

Here is our list of top QBs based on Rider regular seasons in the modern era of the club (from 1946). The list is sorted by total passing yards with the Riders as of the 2009 season.

Name	Rider Years	Rider Yards	%	TDs	Int
1. **Ron Lancaster**	1963-78	46,710	54.2%	299	360
2. **Kent Austin**	1987-93	26,662	57.7%	152	134
3. **Frank Tripucka**	1953-59, 1963	14,387	57.9%	83	119
4. **Tom Burgess**	1987-89, 1994-95	11,852	50.5%	74	74
5. **Joe Paopao**	1984-86	9,337	58.3%	34	63
6. **Henry Burris**	2000, 2003-04	9,004	52.8%	54	43
7. **Nealon Greene**	2002-05	7,968	60.0%	40	26
8. **Reggie Slack**	1997-99	7,754	56.9%	36	37
9. **John Hufnagel**	1980-83, 1987	7,727	56.5%	43	53
10. **Kerry Joseph**	2006-07	7,491	58.0%	46	25
11. **Warren Jones**	1992-96	6,126	53.3%	28	28
12. **Darian Durant**	2006-	5,484	60.3%	31	27
13. **Glenn Dobbs**	1951-53	5,196	50.4%	51	31
14. **Joe Adams**	1982-83	4,841	51.2%	27	22
15. **Bob Ptacek***	1960-65	4,647	54.8%	25	34
16. **Marcus Crandell**	2005-08	4,402	58.0%	24	20
17. **Homer Jordan**	1983-85	4,059	56.1%	21	23
18. **Joe Barnes**	1980-81	3,452	51.9%	20	21

*Ptacek was a linebacker in his final season (1965).

20 Rider Rushing Yardage Leaders

This list includes all-time rushing leaders as of the 2009 season. George Reed is the clear leader of this list.

Name	Rider Years	Rider Yards	Avg yds/ Season
1. **George Reed**	1963-75	16,116	1,240
2. **Mike Saunders**	1992-94, 1997-99	4,396	733
3. **Bobby Marlow**	1953-60	4,291	536
4. **Kenton Keith**	2003-06	3,811	953
5. **Wes Cates**	2007-	3,027	1,009
6. **Bobby Thompson**	1969-74, 1977	2,961	423
7. **Tim McCray**	1986-90	2,898	580
8. **Milson Jones**	1988-92	2,834	567
9. **Ed Buchanan**	1963-67	2,799	560
10. **Steve Molnar, Jr.**	1969-78	2,549	255
11. **Robert Mimbs**	1995-97	2,340	780
12. **Darren Davis**	2000-01	2,267	1,134
13. **Corey Holmes**	2001-05, 2007	2,136	356
14. **Ken Carpenter**	1954-59	2,128	355
15. **Ferdie Burket**	1959-62	2,081	520
16. **Mike Strickland**	1978-79	2,076	1,038
17. **Bill Gray**	1961-65	1,982	396
18. **Silas McKinnie**	1968-71	1,979	495
19. **Chris Szarka**	1997-	1,682	129
20. **Ray Purdin**	1961-63	1,657	552

Great Hands! 36 All-Time Rider Reception Leaders

Here are the top 36 receivers in the modern era of the club (from 1946), including the 2009 season.

Name	Catches	Rider Years
1. **Don Narcisse**	919	1987-99
2. **Ray Elgaard**	830	1983-96
3. **Dan Farthing**	384	1991-01
4. **Jeff Fairholm**	358	1988-93
5. **Chris DeFrance**	328	1981-85
6. **Hugh Campbell**	321	1963-67, 1969
7. **George Reed**	300	1963-75
8. **Joey Walters**	290	1977-82
9. **Bobby Thompson**	266	1969-74, 1977
10. **Tom Campana**	263	1972-77
11. **Alan Ford**	259	1965-76
12. **Matt Dominguez**	250	2003-08
13. **Gord Barwell**	242	1964-73
14. **Mike Saunders**	239	1992-94, 1997-99
15. **Steve Mazurak**	237	1973-80
16. **Jason French**	197	2001-06
17. **Ken Carpenter**	195	1954-59
18. **Craig Ellis**	193	1984-85
19. **Andy Fantuz**	189	2006-
20. **Curtis Mayfield**	182	1996-99

Name	Catches	Rider Years
21. **Travis Moore**	175	2003-05
22. **Milson Jones**	169	1988-92
23. **Corey Grant**	166	2002-08
24. **Corey Holmes**	161	2001-05, 2007
25. **Dwight Edwards**	161	1980-83
26. **Greg Fieger**	154	1980-84
27. **Rhett Dawson**	148	1974-76
28. **Curtis Marsh**	141	2000-01
29. **Elijah Thurmon**	138	2004-05
30. **Harry Lampman**	137	1952-56
31. **Jack Gotta**	132	1960-64
32. **Silas McKinnie**	131	1968-71
33. **Eric Guliford**	128	1999-01
34. **Kenton Keith**	126	2003-06
35. **Stan Williams**	124	1953-57
36. **Jack Hill**	122	1957-61

On a Roll! Winning Streaks of 4 Games or More

Everyone loves a winning streak, and here is a list of Rider winning streaks of four consecutive games or more in a single regular season...

1. **7 Consecutive Wins**
   1969 (last 7 regular season games)
   1970 (last 7 regular season games)

2. **6 Consecutive Wins**
   1928 (undefeated in regular season)
   1934 (undefeated in regular season)
   2008 (first 6 regular season games)

3. **5 Consecutive Wins**
   1919 (undefeated in regular season)
   1931 (undefeated in regular season)
   1968 (the Riders did this twice in the same season)
   1972 (streak ended with Labour Day Classic loss)
   1993 (streak ended with Labour Day Classic loss)
   2005
   2007 (streak ended with Banjo Bowl loss)

4. **4 Consecutive Wins**
   1913, 1914, 1915 (undefeated in regular season)
   1921, 1922 (undefeated in regular season)
   1930 (undefeated in regular season)
   1935 (undefeated in regular season)
   1966
   1967 (twice in same season)
   1976
   1984

In the Dumps – Losing Streaks of 5 Games or More

What goes up often comes down, and here are losing streaks of five or more consecutive games in a single regular season...

1. **12 Consecutive Losses**
   1979 (first 12 regular season games)
2. **10 Consecutive Losses**
   1952
   1959
3. **9 Consecutive Losses**
   1999 (last nine games of the season)
4. **7 Consecutive Losses**
   1948
   1960
   1980
5. **6 Consecutive Losses**
   1978
   1986
   1996
   1998
6. **5 Consecutive Losses**
   1937
   1946
   1985
   1995
   2000
   2001

Who's in Charge?
Riders' Head Coaches 1910-2010

1. **Fred Ritter** – 1910-13
2. **Frank Townsend** – 1914, 1919
3. **Hickory Abbott** – 1915
4. **Heinie Rogers** –1916, 1925
5. **Jerry Crapper** – 1920-21
6. **Jack Eadie** – 1922-23
7. **Pete Dolan** – 1924
8. **Howie Milne** – 1926-28
9. **Greg Grassick** – 1929, 1934
10. **Al Ritchie** – 1930-32, 1935, 1942
11. **Curt Shave** – 1933
12. **Dean Griffing** – 1936-38, 1940-41, 1943
13. **Leo Schweinfurt** – 1939
    (also referred to in some publications as Leo Schweintun)
14. **Don King/Lindsay Holt** – 1945
15. **Ken Preston** – 1946-47
16. **Fred Grant** – 1947-50
17. **Harry Smith** – 1951
18. **Glenn Dobbs** – 1952
19. **Frank Filchock** – 1953-57
20. **George Terlep** – 1958-59
21. **Frank Tripucka** – 1959
22. **Ken Carpenter** – 1960

23. **Steve Owen** – 1961-62
24. **Bob Shaw** – 1963-64
25. **Eagle Keys** – 1965-70
26. **Dave Skrien** – 1971-72
27. **John Payne** – 1973-76
28. **Jim Eddy** – 1977-78
29. **Walt Posadowski** – 1978
30. **Ron Lancaster** – 1979-80
31. **Joe Faragalli** – 1981-83
32. **Reuben Berry** – 1983-84
33. **Jack Gotta** – 1985-86
34. **John Gregory** – 1987-91
35. **Don Matthews** – 1991-93
36. **Ray Jauch** – 1994-95
37. **Jim Daley** – 1996-98
38. **Cal Murphy** – 1999
39. **Danny Barrett** – 2000-06
40. **Kent Austin** – 2007
41. **Ken Miller** – 2008-present

We're # 1! 29 First Place Finishes (West Division)

1. **1911** (3-1)
   Team did not travel to, and forfeited, playoffs in Winnipeg due to claims of bad weather.
2. **1912** (3-1)
   Champs over Winnipeg (West did not play in Grey Cup until 1921).
3. **1913** (4-0)
   Champs over Winnipeg (did not compete in Grey Cup).
4. **1914** (4-0)
   West champs over Winnipeg (did not compete in Grey Cup).
5. **1915** (4-0)
   Champs over Calgary (did not compete in Grey Cup).
6. **1916** (2-0)
   Provincial champs (no interprovincial play due to World War I).
7. **1919** (5-0)
   West champs over Calgary (did not compete in Grey Cup).
8. **1920** (3-0)
   Champs over Calgary and Winnipeg (did not compete in Grey Cup).
9. **1921** (4-0)
   Beat Saskatoon in playoff game on a disputed touchdown, and lost the rematch.
10. **1922** (4-0)
    Lost in playoffs to Edmonton.
11. **1923** (3-1)
    Defeated Edmonton and Winnipeg in playoffs, lost Grey Cup to Queen's University.
12. **1924** (4-2)
    Lost in playoffs to Winnipeg.
13. **1925** (1-0)
    Lost in playoffs to Winnipeg.

14. **1927** (3-0)
Champs over University of BC (did not compete in Grey Cup).

15. **1928** (6-0)
Champs over Winnipeg, lost Grey Cup game to Hamilton.

16. **1929** (3-0-1)
Champs over Calgary, lost Grey Cup game to Hamilton.

17. **1930** (4-0)
Champs over Vancouver, lost Grey Cup to Toronto Balmy Beach.

18. **1931** (5-0)
Champs over Calgary, lost Grey Cup game to Montreal.

19. **1932** (5-1)
Champs over Calgary, lost Grey Cup game to Hamilton.

20. **1933** (5-1)
Lost in playoffs to Winnipeg.

21. **1934** (6-0)
Champs over Vancouver, lost Grey Cup game to Sarnia.

22. **1935** (4-0)
Lost in playoffs to Winnipeg.

23. **1951** (8-6)
Champs over Edmonton, lost Grey Cup game to Ottawa.

24. **1966** (9-6-1)
Champs over Winnipeg, won Grey Cup over Ottawa (first Grey Cup).

25. **1968** (12-3-1)
Lost West Final series to Calgary.

26. **1969** (13-3)
Champs over Calgary, lost Grey Cup game to Ottawa.

27. **1970** (14-2)
Lost West Final series to Calgary.

28. **1976** (11-5)
Champs over Edmonton, lost Grey Cup game to Ottawa.

29. **2009** (10-7-1)
Champs over Calgary, lost Grey Cup game to Montreal.

9 Long Serving Rider Head Coaches

It isn't easy being a Rider head coach, and even harder to be a long serving one...here are nine of the longest serving ranked by seasons as Rider head coach.

1. **Danny Barrett – 7 seasons (2000-06)**
   126 regular games
   D.B. is the longest serving both in terms of seasons and regular season games. He had 57 wins as a Rider coach, second most of all Rider coaches (after Eagle Keys). When Danny Barrett was hired by Roy Shivers in 1999, the Roughriders made history by being the first professional sports team with both a black general manager and head coach.

2. **Eagle Keys – 6 seasons (1965-70)**
   96 regular games
   Keys is the Rider coach with the most wins to date (68 regular season wins) and is arguably the most popular. While with the Riders, Keys coached the team to four first place finishes, four Grey Cup appearances, and its first Grey Cup in 1966. He was voted Coach of the Year in 1968 and inducted into the Canadian Football Hall of Fame as a Builder in 1990.

3. **Dean Griffing – 6 seasons (1936-38, 1940-41, 1943)**
   43 regular games
   Football seasons consisted of eight games when Griffing was brought up from Kansas to coach the Riders in 1936 at the age of 23. He also played centre for the team, and was known as "bad man" because of his hard-hitting playing style. After 1943, he played and coached with Toronto Balmy Beach and Calgary, and then returned as the Riders' general manager from 1953-57. In 1960, he became the first general manager of the Denver Broncos. He was inducted into the Canadian Football Hall of Fame in 1965.

4. **Frank Filchock – 5 seasons (1953-57)**
80 regular games
Filchock had a colourful career prior to becoming the Riders' head coach. As an NFL quarterback in 1939 he threw the first 99-yard touchdown pass in NFL history with the Washington Redskins; and in 1946 led the New York Giants to the NFL title game against the Chicago Bears. On the eve of the game, a radio report rumoured Filchock and another Giant were offered bribes and off-season jobs if Chicago won by more than 10 points. Both players denied it, the Bears only won by 10, but the NFL suspended the two indefinitely. The Hamilton Tigers (not yet the 'Tiger Cats') signed Filchock in 1947, but his application to play was rejected by the league because technically speaking Canadian teams were amateur (not paid professionals). The Tigers were adamant he play and Filchock played two exhibition and four league games (all forfeited in advance) before he was officially allowed to play. In 1950, the NFL reinstated him and he signed with the Baltimore Colts, but they folded at the end of that season. In Canada, he played with Hamilton, Montreal, Edmonton, and Saskatchewan - where his first year as head coach (1953) was his last as a player. After coaching the Riders, he became the first head coach of the Denver Broncos in 1960-1961, under his old Rider GM - Dean Griffing.

5. **Al Ritchie – 5 seasons (1930-32, 1935, 1942)**
19 regular games
Football seasons consisted of four and six games when Al Ritchie coached. He was a figure in Regina's sports scene for 50 years as a coach or manager for amateur hockey and football, and as a coach and general manager of the Riders. Ritchie's Riders rarely lost in the regular season. As Rider manager in the 1920s he presided over several firsts - including a name change from the Regina Rugby Club to the Regina Roughriders, the Riders' first Grey Cup appearance in 1923, and the move to Park de Young (site of what is now Mosaic Stadium/Taylor Field). Ritchie coached and managed the Riders to nine western championships and to the Grey Cup three consecutive years, from 1930 to 1932. Ritchie won national championships in junior football and hockey, but never a Grey Cup, and he died in 1966 before the Riders won their first one. Ritchie was inducted into the Canadian Football Hall of Fame as a Builder in 1963, Canada's Sports Hall of Fame in 1965, the Saskatchewan Sports Hall of Fame in 1966, and the Riders' Plaza of Honor in 1987.

6. **John Gregory – 4+ seasons (1987-91)**
79 regular games
Gregory coached the Riders to their first winning season and playoff appearance in 11 years in 1988, and, after 22 years, their second Grey Cup in 1989. He was voted Coach of the Year in 1989. Midway through the 1991 season, he was released by the Riders (replaced by Don Matthews), but was hired by Hamilton that same season. Since 1995, Gregory has coached in the Arena Football League starting with the Iowa Barnstormers, New York Dragons, Carolina Cobras and Arkansas Twisters, and in 2010 was once again the head coach of the Barnstormers.

7. **Fred Grant – 4+ seasons (1947-50)**
43 regular games
Grant was a fullback with the Alabama Crimson Tide in the years before he became a Rider head coach near the end of the 1947 season. During Grant's time as head coach the Riders officially became the Saskatchewan Roughriders (from the Regina Roughriders) and adopted green and white as their uniform colours (from red and black). Grant coached the team to three second place finishes during his tenure, losing in the Western Final each time to either Calgary or Edmonton.

8. **John Payne – 4 seasons (1973-76)**
64 regular games
Payne coached the Riders to three second place finishes in his first three years as head coach, losing the Western Final every time to the Eskimos. In 1976, the Riders finished first in the West and beat the Eskimos in the Western Final, only to lose the 1976 Grey Cup to the now defunct Ottawa Rough Riders on that heartbreaking touchdown pass from Russ Jackson to Tony Gabriel.

9. **Fred Ritter – 4 seasons (1910-13)**
16 regular games
Credited as the first coach of the team that would become the 'Riders', Ritter captained and played quarter (quarterback) for the team. After going winless in 1910 (losing all four times to Moose Jaw), the team, under Ritter, would lose only twice in the next three years, resulting in three straight first place finishes and two western championships.

4 Short Serving Rider Head Coaches

They say head coaches are "hired to get fired", but some of the shortest serving Rider coaches had other reasons for their seemingly short tenure...

1. **Don King/Lindsay Holt – 1945, 0 regular season games**
   Because of World War II, there were no regular season games in 1945, but the Western Interprovincial Football Union still held playoffs in November of that year. The Riders lost the two game Western Semi-Final series to Calgary by total points of 15 to 1. The Holt-King coaching tandem gave way to Fred Grant the following year, one of the Riders' longest serving coaches.
2. **Heinie Rogers –1916, 1925, 2 regular season games**
   In 1916, most football players everywhere were in the army due to World War I, so the season didn't start until October. Rogers, who also played halfback and quarterback, coached the Regina team to two victories over Saskatoon that month and no other games were played that year. No other games were played in 1917 or 1918 either because of the war. When football resumed in 1919, Rogers continued to play for the team and is credited with being the team's head coach in 1925 when again regular season play was limited, this time due to the lack of teams. That year, the Riders won the provincial championship, but lost in the West Final to Winnipeg.
3. **Frank Tripucka – 1959, 7 regular season games**
   A star Rider quarterback from 1953 to 1959 (third all time leader in many categories), Tripucka asked to be, and was, traded in mid-1959 to Ottawa. He returned in 1959 to be head coach when George Terlep was fired around mid-season. With two games left, Tripucka had to quarterback as well because all of his quarterbacks were injured. A problem was arose because, based on league rules at the time, Tripucka was American and the Riders had a full complement of 12 imports. He quarterbacked both games anyway. The Riders lost to Edmonton 20-19 and beat the Bombers 37-30, but because of Tripucka's ineligibility they had to forfeit both games. The next year, Tripucka left to quarterback the Denver Broncos under his former Rider Head Coach Frank Filchock (and former Rider GM Dean Griffing). He returned in 1963 as a player – a punter and backup quarterback to a young Ron Lancaster.

4. **Walt Posadowski – 1978, 10 regular season games**
   Posadowski was the Riders' offensive line coach when he took over from Jim Eddy for the balance of the '78 season after the Riders went winless in five games. Under Posadowski, the team won four games, lost six, tied another, and finished out of the playoffs for the second consecutive year – after making the playoffs for fifteen straight seasons. The year was also Ron Lancaster's final one as quarterback. The following year, Lancaster took over as head coach.

One Hit Wonders? 9 Single Season Rider Head Coaches

One might think a single season head coach to be less than successful, and for some this was the case; but other single season Rider coaches had modest, and even great, success.

1. **Hickory Abbot –1915, 4-0**
   Finished 1st in West, Western Champs (West did not play in Grey Cup until 1921)
2. **Pete Dolan – 1924, 4-2**
   Finished 1st in West, lost in playoffs to Winnipeg
3. **Curt Shave – 1933, 5-1**
   Finished 1st in West, lost in playoffs to Winnipeg
4. **Leo Schweinfurt – 1939, 6-6**
   Finished 2nd in West, lost in playoffs to Calgary
5. **Harry "Blackjack" Smith – 1951, 8-6**
   Finished 1st in West, Western Champs, lost Grey Cup to Ottawa
6. **Glenn Dobbs – 1952, 3-13**
   Finished 4th in West
7. **Ken Carpenter – 1960, 2-12-2**
   Finished 5th in West
8. **Cal Murphy – 1999, 3-15**
   Finished 4th in West
9. **Kent Austin – 2007, 12-6**
   Finished 2nd in West, Western Champs, Grey Cup Champs

Kick It!
10 Big Kicks in Rider History

Many a game has been decided on a kick, but here are a few of the more famous, and infamous, kicks in Rider history...

1. **November 26, 1989 – "The Kick"**
   77th Grey Cup in Toronto, 43-40 win over Hamilton
   Many feel this was the best Grey Cup ever; it featured the highest total points scored in a Grey Cup (83) and the lead changed three times in the final seconds. The Riders led 40-33 with two minutes to go, and with 44 seconds left, the Ti-Cats tied the game. Rider QB Kent Austin used a hurry-up offence to set up a 33 yard field goal attempt with nine seconds left. After a Ti-Cat timeout, Ridgway split the uprights giving the team its second Grey Cup.

2. **October 14, 1979 – "The Unofficial Start of Rider Pride"**
   26-25 win over Edmonton
   The Riders' 1979 season opened with 12 straight losses under rookie Head Coach Ron Lancaster, and it looked like this game at home on Lancaster's birthday might become the 13th. Edmonton's Dave Cutler was in range for a 32 yard game-winning field goal on the last play of the game, but it went wide. The Riders' Emil Nielsen punted it out to avoid the single, but holder Tom Wilkinson punted it back in. Rider kicker Bob Macoritti fielded Wilkinson's punt and kicked it out, and it again went to Wilkinson, but he went out of bounds. The Riders' victory became a rallying point for Rider Pride Day for the last home game of the season, where an overflow crowd of 28,012 watched the Riders beat the Lions 26-12. Rider Pride was born.

3. **September 4, 1983 – "A Win for Veronica Clark"**
   32-30 Labour Day Win
   The Riders' 1983 regular season opened with a win and then five straight losses, resulting in the firing of popular Head Coach Joe Faragalli. Under new coach Rueben Berry, the Riders lost one more and headed into the Labour Day Classic where they found themselves down 32-29 on the Bomber 41 with 43 seconds remaining, and without Dave Ridgway who suffered a concussion earlier in the game. Rider punter Ken Clark had just returned to Regina for the game from his dying mother's bedside and had not kicked a field goal in seven years. He made it, the Riders won, and his mother Veronica Clark passed away a few hours after the game.

4. **November 30, 1929 – "First Rider Grey Cup Point"**
   17th Grey Cup in Hamilton, 14-3 loss to Hamilton
   In the Riders' first two Grey Cups they failed to score a single point (54-0 in 1923 against Queen's University and 30-0 against Hamilton in 1928), but in their third appearance in 1929 against Hamilton, Saul Bloomington scored a punt single giving the Riders their first Grey Cup point. The game was 2-1 for Hamilton at the half, but Hamilton would go on to win 14-3.

5. **December 6, 1930 – "Almost The First Grey Cup"**
   18th Grey Cup in Toronto, 11-6 loss to Balmy Beach
   In their best Grey Cup in four tries to that point, the Riders came to within an onside kick of winning their first Grey Cup. Despite being denied the use of the forward pass (allowed the previous year), the Riders scored the West's first touchdown and had the ball within Balmy Beach's ten yard line trailing 10-6. The then oft-used onside kick was called, but failed, and the Riders lost 11-6. This was the last year the forward pass was not used in a Grey Cup game.

6. **October 27, 2001 – "Record Setting Field Goal"**
   12-3 win over Edmonton
   The 2001 regular season was a disappointment with the Riders finishing with a 6-12 record; but on this day the Riders would win 12-3 and Rider kicker Paul McCallum would kick a 62 yard field goal that remains the CFL's longest field goal. The record McCallum's field goal beat was Rider Dave Ridgway's 60-yarder kicked in a losing Labour Day classic on September 6, 1987. Ridgway's beat Rider Paul Watson's 59-yarder kicked against Winnipeg on July 12, 1981.

7. **December 2, 1967 – "Record Setting Single"**
   55th Grey Cup in Ottawa, 24-1 loss to Hamilton
   The Riders could not repeat their 1966 Grey Cup winning performance in 1967 against the Hamilton Ti-Cats, scoring only a single point in a 24-1 loss. That single, however, came from an 87 yard punt by Alan Ford and set a CFL playoff record (since surpassed by Lui Passaglia). Though the Riders didn't win, the point kept them from being shutout for a third time in the Grey Cup, and it kept Winnipeg as the last team to be shutout in a Grey Cup game (in 1950).

8. **November 14, 2004 – "Manuregate"**
Western Final, 27-25 OT Loss to BC
The 9-9 Riders finished third in the West Division and knocked off Edmonton 14-6 at Commonwealth Stadium and were poised to beat BC, but gave up a last minute touchdown drive that tied the game and sent it into overtime. In OT, the Riders' Paul McCallum missed an 18 yard field goal and BC ended up winning the game and going to the Grey Cup (losing to Toronto). McCallum's Regina home was vandalized and his family threatened by some misfits. Police charges were laid, and McCallum would leave the team after the 2005 season to play for the Lions.

9. **December 3, 1972 – "Grey Cup Heartbreak"**
60th Grey Cup in Hamilton, 13-10 loss to Hamilton
Like many Rider Grey Cup games, this one came down to the final play of the game. The teams were evenly matched throughout the entire game, which was tied 10-10 from half time up to the final play. With less than two minutes left in the game, Hamilton marched down to the Rider 35 yard line and Ti-Cat Ian Sunter kicked the winning field goal with no time left.

10. **November 29, 2009 – "The 13th Man and the Re-Kick"**
97th Grey Cup in Calgary, 28-27 loss to Montreal
It looked like a major Rider Grey Cup upset and their second Cup in three years. The Riders led 10-0 at the first quarter and 17-3 at the half. However, Montreal pulled to within two points with under two minutes to play and, with 10 second left, missed a field goal attempt from the Riders 43. But, the Riders were called for too many men on the field and the re-kick, from 10 yards closer, was good. It still hurts.

8 Head Coaches with 20 or More Wins *(regular season)*

1. **Eagle Keys** – 68 (1965-70)
2. **Danny Barrett** – 57 (2000-06)
3. **Frank Filchock** – 41 (1953-57)
4. **John Payne** – 40 (1973-76)
5. **John Gregory** – 35 (1987-91)
6. **Don Matthews** – 24 (1991-93)
7. **Ken Miller** – 22 (2008-present)
8. **Fred Grant** – 21 (1947-50)

12 Head Coaches with 20 or More Losses *(regular season)*

1. **Danny Barrett** – 68 (2000-06)
2. **John Gregory** – 43 (1987-91)
3. **Jim Daley** – 36 (1996-98)
4. **Frank Filchock** – 35 (1953-57)
5. **Ron Lancaster** – 28 (1979-80)
6. **Eagle Keys** – 25 (1965-70)
7. **Dean Griffing** – 23 (1936-38, 1940-41, 1943)
8. **John Payne** – 23 (1973-76)
9. **Fred Grant** – 22 (1947-50)
10. **Jack Gotta** – 22 (1985-86)
11. **Don Matthews** – 22 (1991-93)
12. **Joe Faragalli** – 21 (1981-83)

Blowouts For – 10 Rider Shutouts *(30+ points)*

Here is a list of shutouts of 30 points or more recorded by the Riders over other teams in the past 100 years...

1. **47-0**
   October 15, 1949, against the Bombers in Winnipeg
2. **45-0**
   October 13, 1919, at home against the University of Saskatchewan
3. **44-0**
   September 5, 1966, at home against Montreal
4. **40-0**
   October 14, 1922, against the Regina Rowing Club
5. **40-0**
   August 15, 1976, at home against Edmonton
6. **38-0**
   October 15, 1932, in Saskatoon against the University of Saskatchewan
7. **33-0**
   October 27, 1956, at home against Calgary
8. **32-0**
   September 7, 1964, at home against Montreal Alouettes
9. **31-0**
   September 29, 1928, at home against the Winnipeg Tammany Tigers

and oddly enough, one week before...by the identical score...

10. **31-0**
    September 22, 1928 at home against Moose Jaw

...*and Against* – 11 Shutouts Against the Riders (30+ points)

Shutouts of 30 points or more recorded by other teams against the Riders in the past 100 years...

1. **56-0**
   July 5, 1986, in Winnipeg by the Bombers
   (CFL record for highest shutout)
2. **55-0**
   August 24, 1959, in Edmonton by the Eskimos
   (second highest CFL shutout)
3. **42-0**
   October 17, 1964, in Calgary by the Stampeders
4. **40-0**
   September 9, 1979, in Edmonton by the Eskimos
5. **38-0**
   October 29, 1960, in Vancouver by the BC Lions
6. **38-0**
   November 6, 1977, in Edmonton by the Eskimos
7. **38-0**
   October 15, 1910, in Moose Jaw
8. **35-0**
   September 10, 1956, in Winnipeg by the Bombers
9. **34-0**
   August 28, 1954, in Calgary by the Stampeders
10. **32-0**
    September 19, 1959, in Edmonton by the Eskimos
11. **30-0**
    August 17, 1970, in Calgary by the Stampeders

All-Time Rider Interception Leaders

This list includes all-time leaders in interceptions from the modern era (1946) to the end of the 2009 season. Longevity with the Riders plays a part in this statistic, but 'Suits' is the clear leader...

Of special note, with the highest number of interceptions per season played, is Terry Irvin with an average of 8.0 interceptions per season with the Riders. Irvin also played with Calgary and Montreal during his ten year CFL career, and is in 3rd place in the CFL record books for most interceptions in his career at 62. In 1986 while playing for Montreal, Irvin had four interceptions in a game against Toronto, putting him in a tie for second place for the CFL record of most interceptions in a regular season game.

Name	Interceptions	Rider Years	Avg/ Season
1. **Glen Suitor**	51	1984-94	4.6
2. **Ken McEachern**	38	1974-82, 1984	3.8
3. **Bruce Bennett**	35	1966-72	5.0
4. **Ted Dushinski**	33	1965-75	3.3
Steve Dennis	33	1977-78, 1979-84	4.1
5. **Bob Kosid**	32	1964-72	3.6
Albert Brown	32	1987-95	3.6
6. **Gene Wlasiuk**	27	1959-67	3.0
Omarr Morgan	27	2000-06, 2008-	3.0
7. **Harry Skipper**	22	1986-89	5.5
8. **Lorne Richardson**	21	1973-76	5.3
Fran McDermott	21	1982-86	4.2

Name	Interceptions	Rider Years	Avg/ Season
9. **Eddie Davis**	19	2001-09	2.1
Jackie Mitchell	19	2000-06	2.7
10. **Wayne Shaw**	18	1961-72	1.5
11. **Dale West**	17	1962-68	2.4
Mike McGruder	17	1986-88	5.7
12. **Terry Irvin**	16	1984-85	8.0
Eddie Lowe	16	1983-91	1.8
13. **Davin Bush**	15	2001-06	2.5
Terryl Ulmer	15	1993-98	2.5
14. **Larry Dumelie**	13	1960-67	1.6
15. **Paul Williams**	12	1976-78	4.0
Joe Fuller	12	1986-88	4.0
Larry Isbell	12	1954-58	2.4
Bill Manchuk	12	1971-80	1.2
Ted Provost	12	1973-77	2.4
Ventson Donelson	12	1991-00	1.2
16. **Richie Hall**	11	1988-91	2.8
Lance Frazier	11	2006-	2.8
17. **Neil Habig**	10	1958-64	1.4
Harry Lunn	10	1955-58	2.5
Jim Marshall	10	1975-76, 1979	3.3
Billy McBride	10	1980-83	2.5
Bob Ptacek	10	1960-65	1.7

All-Time Rider QB Sack Leaders

This list includes all-time leaders in quarterback sacks at the conclusion of the 2009 season. Bobby Jurasin is the all-time sack leader, and his record will stand for a long, long time. His career total of 142 is third best in CFL history.

Of special note, with the highest number of sacks per season played (14.8), is Vince Goldsmith. Goldsmith won the CFL's Rookie of the Year honour in 1981.

Name	Sacks	Rider Years	Avg/ Season
1. **Bobby Jurasin**	142	1986-97	11.8
2. **Vince Goldsmith**	89	1981-83, 1988-90	14.8
3. **Gary Lewis**	70	1985-94	7.0
4. **George Wells**	53	1974-78	10.6
5. **Scott Schultz**	35	2001-09	3.9
6. **James Curry**	34	1987-89	11.3
7. **Fred Perry**	33	2005-07	11.0
Eddie Lowe	33	1983-91	3.7
8. **Nate Davis**	32	2001-06	5.3
9. **Reggie Hunt**	27	2002-07	4.5
10. **Lybrant Robinson**	25	1994-97	6.3
11. **Dan Rashovich**	23	1987-99	1.8
12. **Shonte Peoples**	22	2001-03	7.3
13. **Rick Mohr**	20.5	1984-85	10.3
14. **Rick Goltz**	20	1984-87	5.0
15. **Terrell Jurineack**	19	2004-07	4.8
Jerald Baylis	19	1992-93	9.5
John Chick	19	2007-09	6.3

Name	Sacks	Rider Years	Avg/ Season
16. **Mike Samples**	18.5	1978-83	3.1
17. **Tim Roth**	18	1971-77	2.6
Lyall Woznesensky	18	1981-82	9.0
18. **Kitwana Jones**	17	2005-08, 2009-	3.4
19. **Jesse O'Neal**	15	1975-76	7.5
20. **Jeff Roberts**	14	1984-85	7.0
21. **Bill Baker**	13	1968-73, 1977-78	1.6
Al Johns	13	1980-87	1.6
Ron Goetz	13	1994-97	3.3
Stevie Baggs	13	2008-09	6.0
22. **Troy Alexander**	12	1995-97	4.0
Demetrius Maxie	12	2000-01	6.0

Bombs Away! Labour Day Match-ups 1936-2009

It's not entirely clear when it started or when it became a Classic, but the Riders and Bombers have met in Regina on or around the Labour Day weekend on a regular basis (but not always annually) since 1936, when Winnipeg's team became known as the "Blue Bombers".

This makes 50 years & 50 games, and the Riders lead the series no matter when you start counting. According to our list, the Riders lead the series 30-20 and are currently on a five game Labour Day winning streak...

1936: **Roughriders 8** - Blue Bombers 7

1939: **Blue Bombers 20** - Roughriders 6

1940: **Roughriders 3** - Blue Bombers 1

1947: **Blue Bombers 6** - Roughriders 5

1948: **Blue Bombers 14** - Roughriders 13
1949: **Roughriders 20** - Blue Bombers 9
1950: **Roughriders 17** - Blue Bombers 2
1951: **Blue Bombers 24** - Roughriders 22
1952: **Blue Bombers 16** - Roughriders 8
1953: **Roughriders 23** - Blue Bombers 19
1954: **Roughriders 18** - Blue Bombers 14
1961: **Blue Bombers 17** - Roughriders 11
1962: **Blue Bombers 30** - Roughriders 7
1963: **Roughriders 15** - Blue Bombers 9
1970: **Roughriders 30** - Blue Bombers 11
1972: **Roughriders 32** - Blue Bombers 21
1974: **Blue Bombers 20** - Roughriders 18
1975: **Roughriders 27** - Blue Bombers 23
1977: **Roughriders 26** - Blue Bombers 18
1978: **Blue Bombers 31** - Roughriders 29
1979: **Blue Bombers 28** - Roughriders 11
1980: **Blue Bombers 32** - Roughriders 29
1982: **Blue Bombers 36** - Roughriders 35
1983: **Roughriders 32** - Blue Bombers 30
1984: **Roughriders 30** - Blue Bombers 25
1985: **Blue Bombers 18** - Roughriders 10
1986: **Roughriders 34** - Blue Bombers 30
1987: **Blue Bombers 29** - Roughriders 25
1988: **Roughriders 29** - Blue Bombers 19
1989: **Blue Bombers 28** - Roughriders 20
1990: **Roughriders 55** - Blue Bombers 11
1991: **Roughriders 56** - Blue Bombers 23
1992: **Roughriders 32** - Blue Bombers 20
1993: **Blue Bombers 25** - Roughriders 24
1994: **Roughriders 42** - Blue Bombers 31
1995: **Roughriders 56** - Blue Bombers 4

1996: **Roughriders 41** - Blue Bombers 23
1997: **Blue Bombers 43** - Roughriders 12
1998: **Roughriders 32** - Blue Bombers 18
1999: **Roughriders 42** - Blue Bombers 17
2000: **Roughriders 38** - Blue Bombers 29
2001: **Blue Bombers 32** - Roughriders 14
2002: **Roughriders 33** - Blue Bombers 19
2003: **Blue Bombers 36** - Roughriders 18
2004: **Blue Bombers 17** - Roughriders 4
2005: **Roughriders 45** - Blue Bombers 26
2006: **Roughriders 39** - Blue Bombers 12
2007: **Roughriders 31** - Blue Bombers 26
2008: **Roughriders 19** - Blue Bombers 6
2009: **Roughriders 29** - Blue Bombers 14

And in case you're wondering about the **Banjo Bowl rematch** in Winnipeg – the series began in 2004 and is currently tied 3-3...

2004: **Blue Bombers 27** - Roughriders 24
2005: **Roughriders 19** - Blue Bombers 17
2006: **Blue Bombers 27** - Roughriders 23
2007: **Blue Bombers 34** - Roughriders 15
2008: **Roughriders 34** - Blue Bombers 31
2009: **Roughriders 55** - Blue Bombers 10

Labour Day Classic 2009
By the Numbers

1 = number of seconds left in the first half after the Riders' goal line stand against the Bombers.

2 = number of yards lost by Bomber Fred Reid on the third and goal play noted above.

3 = interceptions thrown by Bomber quarterback Michael Bishop.

4 = receptions by Rider receiver Weston Dressler.

5 = tackles made by Rider linebacker Tad Kornegay (he also had two interceptions).

6 = tackles made by James Johnson of the Bombers.

7 = points scored by Bomber kicker Alexa Serna.

8 = receptions made by Bomber Terrance Edwards.

9 = points scored by Rider kicker Luca Congi.

10 = points scored by the Riders off the Bombers' four turnovers.

14 = total points scored by the Bombers.

27 = total points scored by the Riders.

41 = rushing yards for Bomber running back Fred Reid.

76 = rushing yards for Rider running back Wes Cates.

246 = passing yards for Rider quarterback Darian Durant.

329 = passing yards for Bomber quarterback Michael Bishop.

30,945 = attendance at Mosaic Stadium (sell out).

982,000 = estimated number of viewers who watched the game on television.

The Big Game!
17 Rider Grey Cup Appearances

The Riders have played in 17 Grey Cups; and as the recaps below show, they've had great plays and players, the weather, and luck (good and bad) influence the outcome...one way or the other...

1. **1923 – December 1, Varsity Stadium, Toronto**
   54-0 loss to Queen's University
   The Roughriders' first appearance in the Grey Cup was an achievement of sorts - the 54-0 loss remains the most lopsided score in a Grey Cup game, and the nine touchdowns scored by Queen's is also a Grey Cup record.

2. **1928 – December 1, Athletic Grounds, Hamilton**
   30-0 loss to the Hamilton Tigers
   After finishing with a 6-0 record in the West, the Riders again failed to score a single point in their second Grey Cup game, although the game was a much closer affair with Hamilton only up by a touchdown at the half. Turnovers did the Riders in, as did former Rider Brian Timmis Sr. who scored two touchdowns for Hamilton. It was the first of five consecutive Rider Grey Cup appearances.

3. **1929 – November 30, Athletic Grounds, Hamilton**
   14-3 loss to the Hamilton Tigers
   In the first ever Grey Cup rematch, the first forward pass in a Grey Cup was thrown by the Riders' Jersey Jack Campbell. The pass was knocked down, but under the rules at the time, the ball was still playable. The rules also made passes within the opposing team's 25 yard line illegal, and Hamilton had one for a touchdown called back.

4. **1930 – December 6, Varsity Stadium, Toronto**
   11-6 loss to Balmy Beach
   In their best Grey Cup result to that point, the Riders were denied the use of the forward pass despite using it the previous year. This was because Balmy Beach did not use the forward pass in its regular season and the league ruled that unless both teams used it, it was banned from Cup play. The Riders scored their first Grey Cup touchdown (and the first by a Western team) when Fred Brown recovered an onside kick in the end zone.

5. **1931 – December 5, Molson Stadium, Montreal**
22-0 loss to the Montreal Winged Wheelers
In the first Grey Cup game played outside Ontario, the forward pass was used by both teams, and effectively by Montreal who scored two touchdowns through the air – the first and second in Grey Cup history. The game is also notable for the Riders' luck when lacrosse shoes ordered by the Riders for better traction on the snow-frozen field were mistakenly delivered to Montreal's dressing room. Montreal used the shoes in the second half, sealing the win.

6. **1932 – December 3, Athletic Grounds, Hamilton**
25-6 loss to the Hamilton Tigers
For the third time in five years the Riders played Hamilton in the Grey Cup, and for the third time they lost. Just like the first time they played the Tigers in 1928, turnovers and former Rider Brian Timmis Sr. did them in. Nonetheless, their fifth consecutive appearance in a Grey Cup would be a record lasting 50 years until the Edmonton Eskimos surpassed it with six, from 1977 to 1982.

7. **1934 – November 24, Varsity Stadium, Toronto**
20-12 loss to the Sarnia Imperials
For the sixth time in seven years, the Riders lost the big game. Sarnia made it to the Grey Cup a few times because league playoff format changes or player eligibility rules made it difficult or undesirable for western teams to challenge for the Cup. However, in 1934 Sarnia was the East Champion and beat the Riders in the big game. It took 17 years for the Riders to get back to the Grey Cup.

8. **1951 – November 24, Varsity Stadium, Toronto**
21-14 loss to the Ottawa Rough Riders
Exactly 17 years to the day from their previous appearance, the Roughriders faced Ottawa in what would be the first of four such match ups before Ottawa's Riders folded after the 1996 season. In the year of "Dobberville" when Saskatchewan finished first under quarterback Glenn Dobbs, a couple of untimely fumbles by halfbacks did Saskatchewan in. Adding insult to injury was the fact star Saskatchewan halfback, Bob Sandberg, was ruled ineligible to play.

9. **1966 – November 26, Empire Stadium, Vancouver**
29-14 win over the Ottawa Rough Riders
After nine attempts and 40 years the Riders finally won their first Grey Cup. Lancaster, Reed, Campbell, West, Ford, Urness and Abendschan, all played major roles in the fourth quarter to help seal the victory.

10. **1967 – December 2, Lansdowne Park, Ottawa**
24-1 loss to the Hamilton Tiger-Cats
The Riders could not repeat in 1967 against Hamilton who were appearing in their eighth Grey Cup game in ten years. The Ti-Cats kept Lancaster to a little over 100 yards in passing and Reed to under 100 yards in rushing; and the rest of the Riders were kept at bay for the entire game. The one point scored by the Riders came from an 87 yard punt by Alan Ford, setting a CFL playoff record.

11. **1969 – November 30, The Autostade, Montreal**
29-11 loss to the Ottawa Rough Riders
In what would be his last game as a player, quarterback Russ Jackson shone as he led Ottawa past an early lead by Saskatchewan and on to the team's second straight Cup. Jackson threw for over 250 yards, had four touchdown passes, ran for another 30 yards, and was the game's MVP.

12. **1972 – December 3, Ivor Wynne Stadium, Hamilton**
13-10 loss to the Hamilton Tiger-Cats
Like many Rider Grey Cup games to come, this one would come down to the final play of the game. The teams were evenly matched throughout the entire game, and it was tied 10-10 from half time up to the final play. With under two minutes left in the game, Hamilton marched down to the Riders' 35 yard line and Ti-Cat Ian Sunter kicked the winning field goal with no time left on the clock.

13. **1976 – November 28, Exhibition Stadium, Toronto**
23-20 loss to the Ottawa Rough Riders
In another Cup decided on the final play, this game was a see-saw battle with Ottawa jumping out to a 10-0 lead after the first quarter, and Saskatchewan leading 17-10 at the half. With less than two minutes left, Saskatchewan prevented Ottawa from scoring with a goal line stand, but Ottawa got the ball back and, with 20 seconds left, Tom Clements threw his unforgettable touchdown pass to Tony Gabriel. It took 13 years for the Riders to return to the big game.

14. **1989 – November 26, SkyDome, Toronto**
43-40 win over the Hamilton Tiger-Cats
In a game many feel was the best Grey Cup, the highest total points ever in a Cup game were scored, and the lead changed three times in the final seconds before a winner was determined. After being behind 13-1 at the end of the first quarter, and 27-22 at halftime, the Riders led 40-33 with two minutes to go. With 44 seconds left, Ti-Cat Tony Champion's spectacular touchdown tied the game, but

Rider quarterback Kent Austin used a hurry-up offence to set up a 33 yard field goal attempt with nine seconds left. After a Hamilton timeout to 'cool' the kicker, Dave Ridgway split the uprights, with what would be known as "The Kick", to give the team its second Cup, 33 years after its first.

15. **1997 – November 16, Commonwealth Stadium, Edmonton 47-23 loss to the Toronto Argonauts**
In a game featuring the 8-10 Riders against the 15-3 Argos, Toronto quarterback Doug Flutie, in his final CFL game, passed for over 350 yards and three touchdowns. The Riders were never in this one, trailing 44-9 in the fourth quarter.

16. **2007 – November 25, Rogers Centre, Toronto 23-19 win over the Winnipeg Blue Bombers**
It was a Labour Day Classic fan's dream – the first ever Grey Cup match-up between the Bombers and the Riders. Both offences struggled, particularly Winnipeg's under quarterback Ryan Dinwiddie, making his first CFL start replacing an injured Kevin Glenn. The Riders' James Johnson had three interceptions, including one with a minute left, sealing the game for the Riders, the team's third Grey Cup. The win made rookie Head Coach Kent Austin the first head coach to win a Grey Cup for the same team for which he won the championship as a quarterback.

17. **2009 – November 29, McMahon Stadium, Calgary 28-27 loss to the Montreal Alouettes**
It was another Rider Grey Cup game decided on the last play, this time by the 13th man in ironic fashion. The Riders led 10-0 after the first quarter and 17-3 at the half. It was looking like a major loss for the Alouettes who lost only three games all season; however, Montreal pulled to within two points, and with 10 seconds left missed a field goal attempt from the Riders 43. The Riders were called for too many men on the field, and the re-kick, from 10 yards closer, was good.

29 Riders in the 1,000 Yard Club

The 1,000 Yard Club informally recognizes running backs, receivers, and returners who reach or surpass 1,000 yards in a single season. Here are 29 Riders in the Club ...

Running Backs

1. **Cookie Gilchrist** – 1958
2. **George Reed** – 1964-69 inclusive, 1971-75 inclusive
3. **Ed Buchanan** – 1964
4. **Mike Strickland** – 1978
5. **Tim McCray** – 1989
6. **Mike Saunders** – 1994
7. **Robert Mimbs** – 1996
8. **Darren Davis** – 2000, 2001
9. **Wes Cates** – 2008

Receivers

10. **Jack Hill** – 1958
11. **Hugh Campbell** – 1964-66 inclusive
12. **Rhett Dawson** – 1975
13. **Chris DeFrance** – 1981-83 inclusive
14. **Joey Walters** – 1981, 1982
15. **Ray Elgaard** – 1985, 1986, 1988, 1990-94 inclusive
16. **Don Narcisse** – 1989-95 inclusive, 1998
17. **Jeff Fairholm** – 1991-93 inclusive
18. **Curtis Marsh** – 2000
19. **Eric Guliford** – 2000
20. **Derick Armstrong** – 2002
21. **Matt Dominguez** – 2003, 2006
22. **Travis Moore** – 2004
23. **Elijah Thurmon** – 2005
24. **D.J. Flick** – 2007
25. **Weston Dressler** – 2008

Returners (kickoffs, punts)

26. **Craig Ellis** – 1984 (kickoff returns)
27. **Willis Jacox** – 1991 (kickoff returns <u>and</u> punt returns)
28. **Corey Holmes** – 2002 (kickoff returns <u>and</u> punt returns)
29. **Corey Holmes** – 2005 (kickoff returns)

Iron Men – 33 Riders Playing the Most Games

This list features 33 all-time leaders in games played as of the conclusion of the 2009 regular season...

Name	Games	Position	Rider Years
1. **Roger Aldag**	271	C/G	1976-92
2. **Gene Makowsky**	248	G	1995-
3. **Ron Lancaster**	246	QB	1963-78
4. **Reg Whitehouse**	238	OT/G	1952-66
5. **Ron Atchison**	237	DT	1952-68
6. **Dave Ridgway**	236	PK	1982-95
7. **Ray Elgaard**	220	SB	1983-96
8. **Don Narcisse**	216	WR	1987-99
9. **Chris Szarka**	206	FB	1997-
10. **Mike Anderson**	205	C/G	1984-95
Dan Rashovich	205	LB	1987-99
11. **Bobby Jurasin**	197	DE	1986-97
12. **Glen Suitor**	194	S	1984-94
13. **Wayne Shaw**	186	LB	1961-72
14. **Jeremy O'Day**	184	OG/C	1999-
15. **Bob Poley**	183	C/T/G	1978-84, 1988-92
16. **Alan Ford**	182	FB/WR/P	1965-76
17. **Vic Stevenson**	172	OT	1983-92, 1998
18. **Paul McCallum**	171	PK	1994, 1995-2005
Gary Brandt	171	G	1967-77
19. **Dan Farthing**	169	SB	1991-2001

Name	Games	Position	Rider Years
20. **Clyde Brock**	159	OT	1964-75
21. **Ted Dushinski**	158	DB	1965-75
22. **Omarr Morgan**	156	CB	2000-06, 2008-
Ralph Galloway	156	OT/G	1969-79
23. **Sully Glasser**	153	FB/QB	1946-57
24. **Gary Lewis**	152	DT	1985-94
25. **Eddie Lowe**	151	LB	1983-91
26. **Gord Barwell**	150	WR	1964-73
Jack Abendschan	150	G/PK	1965-75
27. **Eddie Davis**	145	DB	2001-09
Bill Manchuk	145	LB	1971-80
Lawrie Skolrood	145	TE/OT	1974, 1979-87

Iron Men II – 46 Riders Playing in the Most Seasons

Now, games are one thing, but for this list it's the seasons that count...(including the 2009 season)...

Name	Seasons	Position	Rider Years
1. **Roger Aldag**	17	G/C	1976-92
Ron Atchison	17	DT	1952-68
2. **Ron Lancaster**	16	QB	1963-78
3. **Bill Clarke**	15	DT	1951-64
Gene Makowsky	15	G	1995-
Reg Whitehouse	15	OT/G	1952-66
Freddy Wilson	15	P/RB	1911-16, 1919-21, 1925-30
4. **Ray Elgaard**	14	SB	1983-96
Johnny Garuik	14	OL	1930-43
Tare Rennebohm Sr.	14	G	1916, 1919-31
Dave Ridgway	14	PK	1982-95

Name	Seasons	Position	Rider Years
5. **Sully Glasser**	13	FB/QB	1942, 1946-57
Don Narcisse	13	WR	1987-99
Dan Rashovich	13	LB	1987-99
George Reed	13	RB	1963-75
Chris Szarka	13	FB	1997-
6. **Mike Anderson**	12	C/G	1984-95
Clyde Brock	12	OT	1964-75
Alan Ford	12	FB/RB/P	1965-76
Bobby Jurasin	12	DE	1986-97
Paul McCallum	12	K	1994, 1995-2005
Bob Poley	12	C/T/G	1978-84, 1988-92
7. **Wayne Shaw**	12	LB	1961-72
Vic Stevenson	12	OT	1983-92, 1998
8. **Jack Abendschan**	11	G/PK	1965-75
Gary Brandt	11	G	1967-77
Jerry Crapper	11	TE	1912-16, 1919-24
Ted Dushinski	11	DB	1965-75
Ralph Galloway	11	OT/G	1969-79
Jeremy O'Day	11	C/G	1999-
Glen Suitor	11	S	1984-94
9. **Gord Barwell**	10	WR	1964-73
Al Benecick	10	OT	1959-68
Ken Charlton	10	HB/P	1941,1943, 1945, 1948-54
Andrew Greene	10	G	1997-2006
Bryan Illerbrun	10	T/DT	1978-83, 1986-89
Gary Lewis	10	DT	1985-94
Manchuk, Bill	10	LB	1971-80
Ken McEachern	10	DB/S	1974-82, 1984
Steve Molnar	10	FB	1969-78
Wayne Pyne	10	G/T	1940-41, 1946-53
Lawrie Skolrood	10	TE/OT	1974, 1979-87
Ted Urness	10	C/G	1961-70
Al Urquhart	10	LB	1911-16, 1919-24
Galen Wahlmeier	10	LB/C	1957-62, 1965-68
Don Walsh	10	DT	1955-64

31 CFL Player Records Held by Riders

1. **Most Rushing Attempts, All-Time - 3,243**
   George Reed, 1963-75
2. **Most 1000+ Yard Rushing Seasons, All-Time - 11**
   George Reed, 1963-75
3. **Most Rushing Touchdowns, All-Time - 134**
   George Reed, 1963-75
4. **Most Playoff Rushing Yards, All-Time - 2,584**
   George Reed, 1963-75
5. **Most Playoff Rushing Yards, Single Season - 529**
   George Reed, 1967
6. **Most Playoff Rushing Touchdowns, All-Time - 18**
   George Reed, 1963-75
7. **Most Seasons Catching Passes All Games - 11**
   Don Narcisse, 1987-99
8. **Most Games Catching Passes - 217**
   Ray Elgaard, 1983-96 (Don Narcisse is second with 216)
9. **Most Consecutive Games Catching Passes - 216**
   Don Narcisse, 1987-99
10. **Most 100+ Yard Receiving Games, Regular Season - 11**
    Joey Walters, 1981 (tied with Terry Greer, Hal Patterson, and Alan Pitts)
11. **Most Pass Attempts, Regular Season - 770**
    Kent Austin, 1992
12. **Most Pass Attempts, Game - 65**
    Kent Austin, at home against Edmonton on September 15, 1991 (the Riders lost 41-36)
13. **Most Playoff Passing Yards, All-Time - 6,676**
    Ron Lancaster, 1960-78 (includes his seasons with Ottawa)

14. **Most Playoff Passing Yards, Single Season - 1,273**
Ron Lancaster, 1963 (prior to 1967 the West Semi-Final was a two game total point series, and prior to 1972 the West Final was a best of three series)

15. **Most Playoff Passing Touchdowns, All-Time - 40**
Ron Lancaster, 1960-78 (includes his seasons with Ottawa)

16. **Most Playoff Passing Touchdowns, One Game - 5**
Ron Lancaster, 1963 - The Little Miracle of Taylor Field game - November 11 (Lancaster is tied with Tony Curcillo, Bernie Faloney, Ken Hobart, and Danny Barrett for this record)

17. **Most Passes Intercepted, All-Time - 396**
Ron Lancaster, 1960-78 (includes his seasons with Ottawa)

18. **Most Field Goals, Regular Season - 59**
Dave Ridgway, 1990

19. **Most Consecutive Field Goals, Regular Season - 28**
Dave Ridgway, 1993 (9 games - July 24, 1993 to September 19, 1993, the Riders went 6-3 during the streak)

20. **Most Field Goals, Regular Season Game - 8**
Dave Ridgway did this twice; the first time was against Ottawa on July 29, 1984, and the second was against Edmonton on July 23, 1988 (Ridgway is tied with Mark McLoughlin and Paul Osbaldiston for this record, both of whom did this in 1996)

21. **Most Field Goals, One Quarter - 4**
Dave Ridgway and Paul McCallum have both done this as Riders - Ridgway did it against Calgary at Taylor Field on Oct. 9, 1988 in a 10 minute, 10 second span of the 1st quarter. McCallum did it at home against Edmonton on Sept. 28, 1997 in an unbelievable 4 minute, 27 second span of the 2nd quarter. The Riders won both of these games (Gerry Organ, Dave Cutler, Don Sweet, Lance Chomyc, J.T. Hay, and Terry Baker also share this record, but McCallum and Ridgway are #1 and #2 respectively in terms of the shortest timeframe)

22. **Most Punts, Regular Season Game - 18**
Martin Fabi, against Calgary, September 14, 1963 (the teams played to a 4-4)

23. **Most Punting Yards, Regular Season Game - 814**
Martin Fabi, against Calgary, September 14, 1963 (the teams played to a 4-4 tie)

24. **Most Playoff Punts, Single Season - 46**
Larry Isbell, 1956 (tied with Ron Stewart of Calgary who did this in 1970; prior to 1967 the West Semi-Final was a two game total point series, and prior to 1972 the West Final was a best of three series)

25. **Most Playoff Punting Yards, Single Season - 2,089**
Larry Isbell, 1956

26. **Most Fumble Return Yards, All-Time - 270**
Greg Battle, 1987-98 (Battle played for 5 CFL teams in his 12 seasons in the league, including 1996 as a Roughrider)

27. **Most Interceptions, Rookie Player, Regular Season - 10**
Dale West, 1963 (tied with Bill McFarlane, Harry Skipper, and Steve Muhammad)

28. **Most Interceptions, Rookie Player, Regular Season Game - 3**
Dale West, against Hamilton on August 15, 1963 (the Riders won 5-3; West is tied with Laurent DesLauriers, Bill McFarlane, and Harry Skipper for this record)

29. **Most Quarterback Sacks, Regular Season Game - 5**
Neal Smith, against Calgary on July 7, 1999 (the Riders lost 37-22; ten other players also share this record)

30. **Most Defensive Tackles, All-Time - 1,241**
Willie Pless, 1986 - 99 (Pless played for four CFL teams in his 14 seasons in the league, including his final season - 1999, with the Riders)

31. **Most Defensive Tackles, Regular Season Game - 16**
Reggie Hunt, against Winnipeg on July 10, 2003 (the Riders lost this game 29-27)

II. Off the Field & In the Stands

Were You There?
12 Crowds Over 50,000

Here are the 12 largest crowds, home and away, regular season, playoff and Grey Cup, to have watched the Riders play...

1. **62,517 - September 26, 2009, Commonwealth Stadium, Edmonton**
   Regular season game versus Edmonton. The Riders won 23-20 following a loss to Edmonton at home the week before. It was the largest regular season crowd at Commonwealth, and the second largest crowd ever after the 2002 Grey Cup when Edmonton hosted, and lost to, Montreal.
2. **60,431 - November 16, 1997, Commonwealth Stadium, Edmonton**
   The 1997 Grey Cup game against Toronto; the Riders lost 47-23.
3. **59,723 - August 29, 1982, Commonwealth Stadium, Edmonton**
   Regular season game versus the Eskimos; the Riders won 32-25, but Edmonton went on to the Grey Cup against Toronto and beat the Argos 32-16 to win their fifth straight Grey Cup.
4. **55,438 - October 14, 1995, Taylor Field, Regina**
   Regular season game versus the Stampeders in an expanded Taylor Field. The Riders won 25-20, but Calgary ended up going to, and losing, the Grey Cup against Baltimore at Taylor Field in Regina.
5. **55,227 - November 14, 2004, BC Place Stadium, Vancouver**
   The 2004 Western Final against BC. The Riders lost 27-25 in overtime, and BC went to Ottawa to play in the Grey Cup but lost to Toronto.
6. **54,712 - November 18, 2007, BC Place Stadium, Vancouver**
   The 2007 Western Final against BC. The Riders won 26-17 and went on to win the Grey Cup against Winnipeg in Toronto.
7. **54,088 - November 26, 1989, Skydome (now Rogers Centre), Toronto**
   The 1989 Grey Cup against Hamilton. The Riders won 43-40.

8. **53,467 - November 28, 1976, Exhibition Stadium, Toronto**
The 1976 Grey Cup between the two 'Riders' (the former Ottawa Rough Riders and the 'green & white'); Saskatchewan lost 23-20.

9. **53,216 - October 15, 2006, Commonwealth Stadium, Edmonton**
Regular season game versus the Eskimos; the Riders lost 19-18.

10. **52,230 - November 25, 2007, Rogers Centre, Toronto**
The 2007 Grey Cup against Winnipeg; the Riders won 23-19.

11. **51,448 - August 5, 1983, Commonwealth Stadium, Edmonton**
Regular season game versus the Eskimos; the Riders lost 36-21.

12. **50,540 - October 9, 1977, Olympic Stadium, Montreal**
Regular season game against the original Alouettes; the Riders lost 20-18.

10 Other Rider Record Crowds

1. **Largest Pre-Season Crowd, Mosaic Stadium - 29,107 - June 23, 2009**
The Riders lost to Calgary 27-19, but the regular season would see the team beat Calgary to finish in first place, and to beat Calgary again in the West Final on route to the Grey Cup in Calgary.

2. **Largest Regular Season Crowd, Mosaic Stadium - 55,438 - October 14, 1995**
The Riders beat Calgary 25-20 in a Grey-Cup-expanded Taylor Field, but it was Calgary who ended up going to, and losing, the Grey Cup game against Baltimore at Taylor Field that year.

3. **Largest Labour Day Classic Crowd, Mosaic Stadium - 40,320 - August 31, 2003**
The 2003 Labour Day Classic against Winnipeg; the Riders lost this game 36-18.

4. **Largest Playoff Game Attendance, Mosaic Stadium - 30,945 – Nov. 8, 2008, Nov. 22, 2009**
The first was against the BC Lions in the West Semi-Final where the Riders lost 33-12, the second was the first West Final since 1976 where the Riders beat Calgary 27-17.

5. **Highest Average Rider Home Game Attendance (Regular Season) - 30,717, 2009 season**

6. **Largest Regular Season Crowd at Commonwealth Stadium - 62,517 - Sept. 26, 2009**
   The Riders won 23-20 following a loss to Edmonton at home the week before. It was the second largest crowd ever at Commonwealth Stadium after the 2002 Grey Cup when Edmonton hosted, and lost to, Montreal.

7. **Largest Regular Season Crowd at Winnipeg Stadium - 35,959 - September 12, 1993**
   The Riders lost 41-23; the Stadium's capacity at the time was 33,675. Capacity remained at this level until 1999, when lower deck benches were replaced by theatre-style seats, lowering capacity to 29,533, at which it stands today.

8. **Most-watched Grey Cup - 6.1 million (overall), 8.35 million (peak) - November 29, 2009**
   According to BBM Canada, the industry association involved in broadcast measurement, the 28-27 loss to Montreal was the most-watched telecast of the year in Canada, surpassing both the Academy Awards and Super Bowl XLIII.

9. **Most-watched CFL Playoff Game - 2.2 million - November 22, 2009**
   The Riders' 27-17 West Final victory at home over Calgary averaged two million viewers on TSN, and another 200,000 on French television (RDS). This made the national average audience 2.2 million viewers and surpassed the 2009 East Final between Montreal and BC by over 300,000 viewers.

10. **Most-watched Regular Season Games - 2009**
    At the end of the 2009 regular season, TSN, the CFL's exclusive broadcaster, announced that five of its regular season CFL game broadcasts surpassed one million viewers. Four of these five games involved the Riders:

    - B.C. at Saskatchewan on October 24 (OT) — 1.2 million
    - Edmonton at Saskatchewan on September 20 — 1.1 million
    - Edmonton at Calgary on September 7 — 1.09 million
    - Calgary at Saskatchewan on November 7 — 1.08 million
    - Saskatchewan at B.C. on October 2 — 1.04 million

Rider Cheerleaders (Official & Otherwise)

We all cheer, but some cheer better than others...

1. **Gainer the Gopher**
   Gainer the Gopher has been the team's official mascot since 1977. In his 30+ years of rallying fans and tormenting opposing teams (especially Calgary and Winnipeg), he has developed a fan base as loyal and large as the team's itself. Along the way, he has become a prairie icon, immortalized in print and television commercials.

2. **The 620 CKRM Rider Cheer Team**
   The official Rider cheerleading squad has gone by many names: the Riderettes, Golden Girls, Dream Team, Track and Trail Trailblazers, and others. In addition to sharing game day cheering responsibilities with Gainer, the squad appears at charitable educational and corporate events throughout Saskatchewan. More information about the Cheer Team can be found on the Riders' website.

3. **The 620 CKRM Saskatchewan Roughrider Pep Band**
   The Roughrider Pep Band plays at each home game, in the stands and in front of the stadium before kickoff. It was formed in 1993, and was the first in the CFL, fashioned after U.S. college football team bands. The Pep Band has gone to every Grey Cup since 1993 and is comprised of volunteer musicians who are diehard Rider fans, but also honour other CFL teams by playing their fight songs. The Pep Band's enthusiastic playing actually resulted in a delay of game penalty in a home game against BC *(of all teams !)*.

4. **Cousin Leonard & Gunner the Gopher**
   Gainer is sometimes joined by his cousins Leonard and Gunner. Leonard is officially from Rama, Saskatchewan, and hasn't been seen in awhile, although there is a Bring Back Cousin Leonard page on Facebook. Gunner is the ship mascot for HMCS Regina, and apparently joined Canada's Navy in 1994.

5. **The Flame**
   The Flame (a.k.a. Sandy Monteith) was a fixture at Rider games from the late 1970s to the 1990s. He would light a specially concocted powderkeg in his hard hat after every Rider touchdown. A fan favourite, though insurance and safety issues would move him from the stands to the end zone, to outside the stadium.

6. **The Chicken Man**
   A YouTube, cell phone video and fan favourite – standing out among the green haired, wheat-headed, and melon-headed fans, is The Chicken Man. You can see him dressed in yellow feathers and a Rider jersey, flapping his arms like a chicken at home games.

13 Things You May Not Know about Gainer the Gopher

He's as much a part of the team as anyone, and here are a few things about him you may not know...

1. According to riderville.com, he is one of 38 children born to Dwayne and Agnes Gopher.
2. His birthplace, Parkbeg, Saskatchewan, is 127 km west of Regina on the Trans-Canada Highway #1. According to the Rural Municipality of Wheatlands No. 163, Parkbeg had a population of 12 in 2009.
3. He became the Riders' full time mascot in 1977.
4. Prior to Gainer, the team had no regular mascot and actually used Ralph the Dog – the Calgary Stampeders' mascot, at the 1976 Grey Cup game in Toronto. The idea of using Gainer as the Riders' mascot was conceived during the '76 Grey Cup.
5. In 2006, he was given jersey number 13, as the "13th man", replacing the number 1/2. In 2010, he is wearing #100 in celebration of the Riders' 100th anniversary.
6. "Gainergate - November 5, 2006": Gainer was banned from the Western Semi-Final game played at McMahon Stadium, because the Stampeders said he would detract from their mascot (Ralph the Dog). More likely it was to prevent Gainer from rallying the thousands of Rider fans who would be in attendance. Saskatchewan fans, politicians, and media were solid in their support of Gainer. Calgary received so much negative attention in national and even international press, they backtracked somewhat saying Gainer could sit in the stands but could not be on the field. Gainer chose not to attend. No matter, the Riders beat Calgary 30-21 and moved on to the Western Final. In fact, since banning Gainer, the Stampeders have never beaten the Riders in a playoff game.

7. Gainer has been the subject of other controversy and media attention regarding whether or not he truly is a gopher; and in 2010 the question was whether a rodent-like mascot wearing a green and white jersey in a proposed Super Bowl commercial was a Gainer lookalike or copycat (likely a wannabee).
8. The term 'Gopher' is often (and often incorrectly) used to refer to a number of species in the family Geomyidae in the Rodentia order of mammals. These include ground squirrels, pocket gophers, prairie dogs, and even chipmunks. No one is too sure exactly what Gainer is, but many think he is a Richardson's Ground Squirrel or a Plains Pocket Gopher. This is made even more uncertain by the fact Gainer used to have a longer tail.
9. Richardson's Ground Squirrels can inflict considerable damage on agricultural crops, and farmers in Saskatchewan spend millions of dollars annually to control gophers. In 2009, Saskatchewan's rural municipalities passed a resolution requesting the Richardson's Ground Squirrel be declared a pest under the province's Pest Control Act to allow municipalities to control them in the same manner as rats (baiting, poisoning, trapping fumigating).
10. Gainer made Saskatchewan political history on November 24, 2009, during the Third Session of Twenty-Sixth Legislature, by being allowed on the floor of the Saskatchewan Legislative Assembly as a special citizen (in part because he's unable to fit in the spectators' gallery). He led the members of both political parties in a cheer of Go Riders Go! in support of the Riders' upcoming Grey Cup match in Calgary. It was Gainer's first visit to the Assembly.
11. Gainer is available for public appearances and community events, but he is not available for speaking engagements... because gophers can't speak!
12. At various times, Gainer has been joined on-field by other gopher mascots - Cousin Leonard, Gunner the Gopher (also a cousin, who is in the Canadian Navy and serves on the HMCS Regina) and Goof - a mini-Gainer.
13. G-A-I-N-E-R is an anagram of Regina.

Bottoms Up!
The Riders' 2009 Season in Beer

Beer was first sold at Rider home games in 1992, a season where the Riders went 9-9. Here is the Riders' 2009 season in number of beer sold at Mosaic Stadium...

1. **20,487 – Tuesday, June 23, 2009**
   (pre-season game – Riders lost to Calgary 27-19)
2. **31,289 – Friday, July 3, 2009**
   (Riders beat BC 28-24)
3. **31,519 – Saturday, July 18, 2009**
   (Riders lost to Montreal 43-10)
4. **34,861 – Saturday, July 25, 2009**
   (Riders lost to Edmonton 38-33)
5. **17,018 – Sunday, August 16, 2009**
   (Riders beat Hamilton 33-23)
6. **44,479 – Sunday, September 6, 2009**
   (Labour Day Classic – Riders beat Winnipeg 29-14)
7. **21,193 – Sunday, September 20, 2009**
   (Riders lost to Edmonton 31-27)
8. **13,705 – Saturday, October 10, 2009**
   (Riders beat Toronto 32-22)
9. **22,714 – Saturday, October 24, 2009**
   (Riders beat BC in OT 33-30)
10. **27,740 – Saturday, November 7, 2009**
    (Riders beat Calgary 30-14 to finish in first place in the West)
11. **32,718 – Sunday, November 22, 2009**
    (West Final – Riders beat Calgary 27-17)

Note: Over 250 volunteers per game are involved in food and alcoholic beverage sales for charity fundraising, and the total amount donated by the Riders to youth oriented charities from the proceeds of these sales in 2009 was $407,356.

Source for beer sales: Saskatchewan Roughrider Food Services

Chow Down! Food & Drink by the Numbers (2009 season)

2	=	thousands of pounds of popcorn seed popped.
51	=	thousands of packets of mustard spread on hot dogs, hamburgers, smokies, bratwurst and pretzels.
106	=	number of 4 litre jars of sauerkraut consumed.
116	=	number of 4 litre jars of sliced dill pickles consumed.
216	=	thousands of napkins by fans' to keep their faces clean.
250	=	volunteers per game involved in food and alcohol beverage sales for charity fundraising.
1,200	=	gallons of hot chocolate consumed.
1,235	=	pounds of onions diced up for the condiment stands.
1,920	=	packages of licorice sold.
2,869	=	number of dozen hot dog buns used.
3,158	=	number of dozen hamburger buns used.
4,800	=	packages of sunflower seeds sold.
8,750	=	number of soft, super pretzels sold.
33,768	=	number of bottles of water sold at stadium concessions.
34,304	=	process cheese slices used to top up those cheeseburgers.
34,430	=	hot dogs sold (not including smokies or bratwurst).
37,895	=	number of burgers consumed.
46,488	=	bottles of soft drinks sold at stadium concessions.
93,300	=	pounds of ice used.
162,733	=	alcohol drinks sold (not including beer).
287,723	=	beer sold (pre-season, regular season and West Final).
407,356	=	dollars donated by the Riders to youth oriented charities from the proceeds of food and alcoholic beverage sales.

Source: Saskatchewan Roughrider Food Services

5 Rider Cheer Songs

Also called 'fight songs', here are five Rider cheer songs and their lyrics fans may (or may not) know by heart. (For pop songs see the list "Riders on the Charts")

1. **"On Roughriders!"**
   This cheer song is an adaptation of "On Wisconsin" composed in 1909 by William T. Purdy originally for the University of Minnesota. Carl Beck, an alumnus of the University of Wisconsin convinced Purdy to allow his alma mater to use it. Beck wrote the football-oriented lyrics and changed Minnesota to "On, Wisconsin!" In 1968, Canadian big band leader Dal Richards adapted the lyrics for an album of Canadian Football Songs. The song is in the public domain in North America and is used by the State of Wisconsin.

   On Roughriders, on Roughriders,
   Plunge right through that line.
   Rider fans are all behind you,
   Touchdown every time.
   On Roughriders, on Roughriders,
   Fight on for your fame.
   Fight, fellas, fight
   And we will win this game.

2. **"Green is the Colour"**
   This unofficial anthem was adapted from Blue Is the Colour, a song associated with, and performed by, the United Kingdom's Chelsea Football Club (soccer) in 1972 to coincide with the club's appearance in its league final. Their song actually reached the UK music charts staying on for 12 weeks, reaching number 5 in March 1972. It was adapted for the Riders by Steve Mazurak, former Rider player and the team's current Vice-President of Marketing and Sales, and his wife. The cheer song has also been adapted by the Vancouver Whitecaps ("White is the Colour") and a number of European soccer teams.

   Chorus: Green is the colour, football is the game,
   We're all together, Winning is our aim,
   So cheer us on through the sun and rain,
   Saskatchewan Roughriders is our name.

Let's show our pride for the Green & White,
We will fight, green and white,
Sing loud and long til the game is won,
The best is yet to come.

Here at Taylor Field we are number one,
We're the best, east or west,
We'll give our all til the game is won,
Stand up and sing everyone.

3. **"Rider Pride"**

"Rider Pride Day" was October 28, 1979, against the BC Lions. It was the last home game of the season and the Riders had only one win to that point. The promotion was a huge success, with an overflow crowd (28,012) and a Rider win (26-12). Since then, Rider Pride has been part of the Rider vocabulary and the song is often heard.

We're really rollin', now we're on our way
Our Pride is showin', ya it's growin' everyday

Chorus: We've got that Rider Pride
A feeling deep inside
Its Rider Pride, Rider Pride
We got that Rider Pride
You know we just can't hide that Rider Pride

We're ridin' high now, headin' for the top
We've got a winner, ya we're givin' all we got

4. **"Green, White, Fight, Fight, Fight"**

According to the Rider Pep Band website, this cheer is sung to the tune of "Bear Down Arizona," the cheer song of the Arizona Wildcats of the University of Arizona in Tucson. It was composed in 1952 by Jack K. Lee, the university's band director. How it got adapted for the Riders and by whom is uncertain.

Let's cheer for our Riders,
Let's cheer, green & white,
Let's cheer for our Riders,
Show our team that their fans have pride.
Let's cheer for our Riders,
Let's cheer, green & white,
Green, white, fight, fight, fight,
Bring a victory home tonight.

5. **"Saskatchewan Tough"**

"Saskatchewan Tough" coincided with the hiring of Head Coach Reuben Berry (replacing Joe Faragalli) mid-season in 1983. Berry, who served in the U.S. military, coined the term Saskatchewan Tough, but it is uncertain who wrote the cheer song for the Riders.

When the going gets rough
We don't mind it
Cause that's when the Tough get going
We dig down deep we get behind it
our Rider Pride starts show'n

We're Saskatchewan Tough
We've got the right stuff
Go'in all the way
We never give in
We never give up
We're Saskatchewan Tough
We're Saskatchewan Tough

We've got what it takes
We can do it
If we all pull together
We know we can win
There's nothin' to it
We just keep get'in better

Green Wasn't Always The Colour! Rider Uniform Colours

It's hard to picture, but yes, the Riders didn't always wear the ol' green & white...here are the team uniform colours through the years...

1. **Gold & Purple – 1910 (Regina Rugby Club)**
2. **Blue & White – 1911 (Regina Rugby Club)**
3. **Red & Black – 1912-47 (Regina Rugby Club/ Regina Roughriders/Saskatchewan Roughriders)**
   Apparently adopted for the colours of the Canadian infantry contingent that fought with Teddy Roosevelt in the Spanish-American war; this is also one of the potential reasons for the adoption in 1924 of the name – Roughriders.
4. **Green & White – 1948-85**
   Rider lore has it the team was in bad need of uniforms when an executive of the club (Jack Fyffe) found a set of green and white jerseys at a surplus store in Chicago. The rest, as they say, is history.
5. **Green & White, and Black & Silver – 1985 to present**
   When the Roughriders updated their logo to feature the stylized "S", they also added black and silver trims to the team's green and white colours.
6. **Red & Black – 2010 (retro jerseys)**
   As part of the team's 100th centennial, the Riders once again sported the red & black jerseys they wore from 1912-47 in a game against the Edmonton Eskimos on July 17, 2010, at Mosaic Stadium.

Taylor Field/Mosaic Stadium Through the Years

The *current* home of the Riders has a history as old as the team itself, and here are a few milestones...

1910 - Park Hughes rugby field constructed on present-day site. The Regina Rugby Club plays and practices here as well as at Railway Park, Dominion Park, and Exhibition Park until 1928.

1927 - Park Hughes and the adjoining Park de Young reconfigured into one facility called Park De Young.

1928 - Park de Young becomes the official home of the Roughriders.

1929 - Site of the first interception return for a touchdown in Canadian football when Rider Fred Brown intercepted a Calgary Tigers pass in the Western Final.

1936 - Press box built for radio broadcasts, additional bleachers added.

1946 - Field seeded to provide turf surface, prior to this topsoil was added each season.

1947 - Park de Young renamed to Taylor Field in honour of N.J. "Piffles" Taylor, Rider player, executive and president who died in 1946. Taylor also sat on Regina City Council from 1924-29.

1948 - 4,500 seat grandstand built on the west side at a cost of $47,000. First home playoff game of the "Saskatchewan" Roughriders (team was the Regina Roughriders until 1946). Riders tie Calgary 4-4 in the first of a two game total point series (Calgary wins second game at home 17-6).

1951 - Riders win two games at home in best-of-three West Final after losing game one in Edmonton, and advance to the Grey Cup for the first time since 1934. First time a CFL field is covered as 375 truck tarps are laid down to protect the field from driving rains.

1963 - "The Little Miracle of Taylor Field" - in the two game total points Western Semi-Final, the Riders lose 35-9 in Game 1 in Calgary, but win by 27 points at home (39-12) when Lancaster throws a CFL playoff record five touchdown passes (record still stands).

1978 - Second level added to West Side grandstand - capacity is 27,637.

1979 - First artificial turf installed. The last home game is designated "Rider Pride Day" - 28,012 fans watch the Riders beat the BC Lions 26-12 to finish at 2-14.

1983 - City of Regina is given the legislative authority to sell liquor at Taylor Field, but it takes nine more years and much discussion and debate for beer to finally be sold (in 1992).

1988 - First artificial turf replaced with OmniTurf, inlaid with sand, at a cost of about $850,000.

1995 - $1.3 million expansion to accommodate the 1995 Grey Cup sees the addition of the eastside club seating area. Largest home crowd ever (55,438) watched the Riders beat Calgary 25-20 on October 14. On November 19, 52,564 people watched the Baltimore Stallions beat the Stampeders 37-20 to become the first and only US-based CFL team to win the Grey Cup.

2000 - OmniTurf replaced with AstroTurf at a cost of about $2 million.

2003 - Second Grey Cup game held at Taylor Field - 50,909 watched Edmonton beat Montreal 34-23.

2005 - SaskTel MaxTron was installed at a cost of $1 million.

2006 - The Riders, with approval of the City of Regina, enter into a 10 year $3.75M sponsorship with Mosaic Canada that sees the facility renamed "Taylor Field at Mosaic Stadium" The stadium hosts two Rolling Stones concerts on October 6th and 8th attended by over 80,000 people.

2007 - FieldTurf replaces AstroTurf. The stadium hosts the first home playoff game since 1976. The Riders defeat Calgary 26-24 in the West Semi-Final in front of a capacity crowd of 28,800, on their way to what would be their third Grey Cup victory.

2008 - All Rider home games sell out and 2,145 temporary seats are added in time for the Labour Day Classic, bringing the seating capacity to 30,945. The seats return for the entire 2009 season.

2009 - The stadium hosts the West Final for first time since 1976 and 30,945 fans watched the Riders beat Calgary 27-17 and head to the Grey Cup against Montreal.

2010 - A feasibility study into a multi-purpose entertainment facility to replace Mosaic Stadium places the cost of a 33,000 seat (for football) facility with a retractable roof at over $431 million.

Taylor Field/Mosaic Stadium By the Numbers

1 = rank of the two Rolling Stones' concerts held at Mosaic Stadium in October 2006 among the top grossing concert events all time in Canada by Pollstar magazine.

1.50 = Riders' game ticket prices in 1948.

2 = number of facilities reconfigured in 1927 to create what would later be named Taylor Field/Mosaic Stadium (Park Hughes and Park de Young).

2.66 = average occupancy (passengers) per car at the October 24, 2009, game against BC (the Riders won in overtime 33-30) according to a survey by the City of Regina.

4 = artificial turf systems installed to date (Super Turf/Tartan Turf, OmniTurf, AstroTurf, FieldTurf).

6 = number of the ten longest field goals in CFL history kicked at Taylor Field/Mosaic Stadium.

8 = field goals kicked by Dave Ridgway in a July 23, 1988 game against Edmonton.

12 = millions of dollars grossed by the Rolling Stones' concerts held at Mosaic Stadium in 2006.

15 = section in which no alcohol is permitted.

18 = consecutive sellouts over the 2007 and 2008 seasons.

46 = number of buses (Football Express and private charters) parked on site on game days.

65 = dollars for an adult, non-Labour Day regular game ticket seated between 45-55 yard lines.

72 = dollars for an adult, Labour Day Classic game ticket seated between 45-55 yard lines.

101 = longest punt (yards) kicked by a Rider at Taylor Field – Ken Clark vs Winnipeg, Sept. 3, 1963.

102 = longest punt (yards) kicked by anyone at Taylor Field (by Dave Mann of the Toronto Argonauts against the Riders on Sept 18, 1966 – second longest punt in CFL history).

104 = total points scored on July 28, 2000, in a regular season game between Calgary and Saskatchewan (game tied at 52-52), third highest in CFL history.

300 = tons of sand that held down the OmniTurf inlay artificial turf system installed in 1988.

375 = truck tarps laid down to protect the field during the 1951 West Final.

1,000 = approximate number of non-spectator staff, media, security, vendors and volunteers on-site during a regular season Rider home game in 2009.

1,706 = estimated number of people arriving at Rider regular season games by transit.

2,145 = temporary seats added in time for Labour Day Classic in 2008, and for entire 2009 season.

27,637 = official seating capacity in 1985 according to the 1985 Rider Club Directory (media guide).

28,800 = official 'capped' seating capacity in 2008, before temporary seating was added.

29,107 = largest pre-season game attendance, June 23, 2009, against Calgary (Calgary won 27-19).

30,945 = seating capacity for the entire 2009 season with the temporary seats added.

55,438 = largest home crowd – Oct. 14, 1995, regular season game against Calgary (Riders won 25-20).

65,860 = litres of water consumed during the October 24, 2009, regular season game against BC.

80,583 = total attendance for the Rolling Stones' concerts held on October 6th and 8th in 2006.

200,000 = maximum annual lease payment by the Riders to the City of Regina for use of the stadium.

375,000 = dollars paid annually by the Mosaic Company for stadium naming rights from 2006 to 2015.

Green is so the Colour! 10 Highest 50-50 Prize Payouts

The annual Labour Day game against Winnipeg is famous...or is that infamous...for many reasons, so it's no surprise the largest 50/50 payouts of the year are on Labour Day Classic game days. Here are the top ten payouts for each of the last ten years...

1. **September 6, 2009 - $41,763** (Riders won 29-14)
2. **August 31, 2008 - $41,695** (Riders won 19-6)
3. **September 2, 2007 - $39,356** (Riders won 31-26)
4. **August 31, 2003 - $39,007** (Riders lost 36-18)
5. **September 3, 2006 - $31,777** (Riders won 39-12)
6. **September 5, 2004 - $29,039** (Riders lost 17-4)
7. **September 4, 2005 - $28,336** (Riders won 45-26)
8. **September 1, 2002 - $27,969** (Riders won 33-19)
9. **September 3, 2000 - $23,333** (Riders won 38-29)
10. **September 2, 2001 - $22,831** (Riders lost 32-14)

Source for 50/50 payouts: University of Regina Rams Football Club

Riders' General Managers (*modern era*)

Throughout the club's history, many former (and active) players and team supporters took on management roles. This list includes GMs from the club's modern-era.

1. **Clair Warner (1946-49, 1951-52)**
   Warner came to Regina from South Dakota and began playing (as an "end") for the Riders in 1919. He served the team in various capacities over approximately 50 years. He played in four Grey Cups, and served as a club director, president, and general manager.

2. **Greg Grassick (1950)**
   Grassick's association with the Riders began in the 1920s. Greg served several roles with the Riders: player (halfback), coach, and executive member. He also played for McGill University in 1925. His father, James Grassick, was a founding father of the City of Regina, elected to the council and twice as mayor of the City, and he was also elected to the Saskatchewan Legislative Assembly.

3. **Frank Filchock (1953)**
   Filchock had a busy year in 1953, playing quarterback (58.5%; 925 yds; 5 TDs; 7 Ints), and serving as head coach (1953-57) and general manager. Before coming to the CFL, Filchock played eight seasons (1938-41, 1944-46, 1950) in the NFL with (Pittsburg, Washington, New York Giants, and Baltimore). When he played for the New York Giants his head coach was Steve Owen; Owen went on to be the Riders' head coach in 1961-62. Before joining the Riders in 1953, Filchock played in the CFL with Hamilton (1947-48), Montreal (1949-50), and Edmonton (1951-52). In case you were wondering about the gap in Filchock's NFL playing days, he was suspended from 1947-50 as a result of a famous gambling scandal involving the 1946 NFL Championship game. Although Filchock had been offered a bribe, in the end a judge found he was not an accomplice in the scandal, but was rather a victim of unfortunate circumstances. The outcome didn't matter to NFL Commissioner, Bert Bell, who suspended Filchock, only to agree in 1950 to reinstate him. It was during the period of his ban from playing in the NFL he first came to play in the CFL. After his playing days Filchock went on to become the first head coach (1960-61) of the newly formed Denver Broncos.

4. **Orin D. "Dean" Griffing (1954-57)**
Griffing, Kansas State University Class of 1936, came to Regina that same year to be the Riders' head coach, but an injury to a player resulted in his playing centre. As a player he earned the nickname "Bad Man" because of his bruising style of play. Griffing is credited with playing (1936-41), and serving as head coach (1936-38, 1940-41, 1943), in addition to becoming the general manager. After his time with the Riders, Griffing became the first general manager of the newly established NFL Denver Broncos. It was said that in the Broncos inaugural years they not only played poorly, they looked bad because of the uniforms they wore. Bronco quarterback (and former Rider quarterback) Frank Tripucka said of Griffing, ". . . we called him Mr. Moustache and any owner would love him because he was a real penny-pincher." Griffing is an All-time Letterman (centre, 1933-34) with the Kansas State Wildcats football team, and was the team's captain in 1935.

5. **Ken Preston (1958-78)**
Preston made an immense contribution to the Rider organization. He was a quarterback (1940, 1943, 1946-48), head coach (1946-47), and then general manager for about two decades. Other stops as a player in the CFL included Winnipeg and Ottawa. Preston's son, Rich, born in Regina, Saskatchewan, played eight seasons in the National Hockey League (six with Chicago and two with New Jersey.) Rich Preston has coached in the NFL for about 15 seasons. Rich is the general manager and head coach of the Lethbridge Hurricanes of the Western Hockey League.

6. **Henry (Hank) Dorsch (1978-79)**
Born in Saskatchewan, Dorsch played with the Regina Rams for two seasons before a football scholarship took him to the University of Tulsa, Oklahoma. Dorsch led the Tulsa Golden Hurricane in rushing in 1962 (56 carries; 250 yds; 4.5 yd avg; 2 TDs) and 1963 (48 carries; 211 yds; 4.4 yd avg; 3 TDs). Dorsch's head coach at Tulsa was none other than popular Rider Quarterback (1951-53) Glenn Dobbs. After university, Dorsch joined the Riders for eight seasons (fullback, defensive back, 1964-71). He played in three Grey Cup games, and was on the 1966 team that won the Riders' first Grey Cup. Outside of the Riders, Dorsch worked at the Regina General Hospital and for the Government of Saskatchewan.

7. **Jim Spavital (1980-82)**
A product of Oklahoma State, Spavital was the 11th pick in the 1st round of the 1948 NFL draft by the Chicago Cardinals. He is credited with two seasons in the NFL with the then Los Angeles Dons (1949) and the Baltimore Colts (1950). Spavital played in the CFL for one season; 1951 with the Winnipeg Blue Bombers as a fullback. He first joined the Riders as an assistant coach (1968-69) under legendary Rider head coach Eagle Keys (1965-70). After leaving Saskatchewan, Spavital took on the head coaching job with Winnipeg from 1970-73. He was also an assistant coach with Calgary in 1978-79. After leaving Calgary, Spavital became the Riders' general manager for three seasons. Spavital also coached in the U.S. college and other now defunct professional football leagues. Spavital was a standout fullback for Oklahoma in the 1945 Cotton Bowl against Texas Christian University Horned Frogs on New Year's Day in Dallas, Texas in front of 37,500 fans. Spavital had 119 yards (52 longest) on the day as he helped his team to a 34-0 win.

8. **John Herrera (1983-84)**
Herrera began a long affiliation with NFL's Oakland Raiders in 1963 at the behest of then and still Raiders' owner Al Davis. John's father Andy Herrera owned a car dealership (Herrera Buick) in Oakland and was a sponsor of the Raiders. These connections led to a young John getting summer employment in the Raiders' front office. Aside from a two season stint as the Riders' GM, Herrera returned to the NFL and the Raiders, where he continues as a Senior Executive in public/community relations.

9. **William H. "Bill" Quinter (1985-86)**
Quinter played football with the Indiana University Hoosiers in 1960-61, going on to play four seasons in the CFL in Ottawa (end) from 1962-65. Other CFL posts included: assistant coach with Toronto from 1973-75, assistant coach with Calgary in 1976, and assistant coach with British Columbia from 1977-82. Quinter was also a player scout for several NFL teams during his career. The Riders' head coach during Quinter's tenure was Jack Gotta. Both Quinter and Gotta were released after serving two of their three year contracts, and after their departure it was rumoured the club continued to pay for the last year of the contracts.

10. **Bill Baker (1987-88)**
Baker attended Otterbein College in Ohio where he played football for four seasons. He received accolades from the Ohio Athletic Conference for playing tackle in 1965-66 and linebacker in 1967. From college he moved to Regina for employment with the City of Regina's tourist bureau. He went on to play for the Riders where he became a ferocious pass rusher (defensive end, 1968-1973, 1977-1978) giving him the nickname "The Undertaker." He also played three seasons in British Columbia (1974-76). Baker's nickname surely was inspired by the song "Old Bill Baker [the Undertaker]" (lyrics by Ring Lardner) of the Jerome Kern Broadway musical comedy "*Very Good Eddie*" (1915, revived 1975).

11. **Alan Ford (1989-99)**
Ford, born in Regina, attended the University of the Pacific in California (College of the Pacific Class of 1965) on a basketball scholarship. He returned to Saskatchewan to play for the Riders (fullback, wide receiver, punter, from 1965-76). After his playing days he joined the Riders' management as an assistant coach in 1979, and ten years later as general manager (1989-99). During a difficult period for the CFL in 2003 when the Hamilton Tiger Cats were on the verge of folding, Ford was brought in by the league as the interim general manager of the Hamilton Tiger Cats, where Rider legend Ron Lancaster was the head coach. Ford was inducted into the Saskatchewan Sports Hall of Fame in 2010.

12. **Roy Shivers (2000-06)**
Following a stint in the U.S. Army, Shivers went to Utah State where he was a star running back, receiving All-American honours in 1965. Among his many records in the Utah State football record book, Shivers is tied for the season scoring record with 16 TDs in 1965, is third in all-time yards per carry at 6.8 in 1964-65, and is tied for third place for the most points in a season at 96. After college, Shivers was drafted into the NFL and played for seven seasons (1966-72) with the St. Louis Cardinals. After his playing days, he went to coach football at several U.S. universities before moving to the CFL. Shivers came to the CFL as an assistant coach in British Columbia from 1983-86, assistant general manager with Calgary from 1991-94, general manager in 1995 of the short-lived U.S. expansion team in Birmingham, and then back to Calgary as the assistant general manager from 1996-99. Shivers became in 2008 the director of player personnel for British Columbia.

13. **Eric Tillman (2007-09)**
A graduate of the University of Mississippi, Tillman's football career includes various administrative positions in the NFL and NFL Europe. Prior to joining the Riders, his other stints in the CFL included Montreal (player personnel) in 1981-82, general manager for the British Columbia Lions from 1993-95, general manager for the Toronto Argonauts in 1999, and the general manager in Ottawa from 2003-05. He was also a football broadcast analyst and scout for various teams. During Tillman's tenure the team made it into the Grey Cup game twice, winning in 2007.

14. **Brendan Taman (2010-)**
Taman, a native of Saskatoon, Saskatchewan, got his start in the CFL, unofficially at least, at the Riders' 1982 training camp in Saskatoon where he apparently held the ball for the legendary Dave Ridgway. Officially, Taman joined the CFL as a player personnel assistant with the Riders from 1987-89 before moving on to be the manager of football operations in Ottawa from 1989-92. Taman returned to the Riders from 1993-96, again in a player personnel role, and then a similar role in British Columbia from 1997-99. He then stepped it up by becoming the assistant general manager in Winnipeg from 1999-2001, and then Winnipeg's general manager from 2004-09. In early 2009, Taman resigned from Winnipeg, and by mid-2009, Taman left Winnipeg and joined the Riders in the role of director of football administration. Taman became the Riders' general manager in January 2010.

Riders' #1 & First Round CFL Draft Picks

1. **2010 – Shomari Williams, Defensive End**
   With its first overall pick in almost ten years, the Roughriders made Queen's University defensive end Shomari Williams its #1 pick in the 2010 CFL Canadian Draft, obtaining the first overall pick in a trade with the Argonauts.

2. **2001 – Scott Schultz, Defensive Tackle**
   The 2001 CFL Draft saw the Riders with its second consecutive first overall pick, selecting Schultz out of the University of North Dakota. Schultz missed the first half of back-to-back seasons (2001 and 2002) due to stints with San Diego & Pittsburgh in the NFL. Schultz recorded 178 tackles and 35 sacks with the Riders. Schultz retired after five games into the 2009 season.

3. **2000 – Tyson St. James, Linebacker**
   Selected first overall out of the University of British Columbia, St. James played with the Riders from 2000-02, before moving on to the Winnipeg Blue Bombers for a year.

   Other First Round Rider Picks

Year	Name	Pick	Position	Rider Years
1986	**Rueben Mayes**	2	RB	n/a
1988	**Jeff Fairholm**	2	SB	1988-93
1988	**Pete Giftopolous**	6	LB	n/a
1989	**Kevin Smellie**	2	RB	n/a
1989	**Andrew Thomas**	3	DB	n/a
1989	**Donovan Wright**	4	DB	1989
1990	**Glen Scrivener**	3	DL	1990-91
1990	**Dane McArthur**	8	SB	1991-93
1991	**Dan Farthing**	2	SB	1991-2001
1991	**Paul Vajda**	5	OG	1991-96
1992	**Mark Scott**	2	LB	1992
1993	**Brad Elberg**	2	RB	n/a
1994*	**Chris Burns**	2	OL	1994-95
1994*	**Matthieu Quiviger**	10	OL	n/a

Year	Name	Pick	Position	Rider Years
1995*	**Troy Alexander**	4	DT	1995-97
1995*	**Dwayne Provo**	10	DB	1995-96
1995*	**Rob Lazeo**	12	OL	1997-98,2002-06
1996	**Mike Sutherland**	3	OG	1996
1997	**Ben Fairbrother**	2	OL	1997-2000
1998	**Curtis Galick**	7	DB	1998-99
2004	**Ducarmel Augustin**	6	FB	2004
2005	**Matt O'Meara**	3	OL	2005-06
2005	**Chris Best**	4	OL	2007-
2005	**Nathan Hoffart**	7	SB	2005-07
2006	**Andy Fantuz**	3	SB	2006-
2008	**Keith Shologan**	4	DL	2008-

n/a = not applicable (did not play in a Rider regular season game)
* these years had a Bonus Round before the First Round

U.S. University/College Source of Most Rider Alumni

Our research suggests the University of Utah football program is the U.S. university/college source of the most Riders. The "Utes" compete in the Mountain West Conference of the Football Bowl Subdivision of NCAA Division I. The Utah football program began in 1892.

Name	University	Position	Rider Years
1. **Marvin Beguhl**	Utah	DE	1954
2. **Armand Boglin**	Utah	LB	2001-02
3. **Ron Cherkas**	Utah	DT	1976-80, 1982, 1985
4. **Norm Chow**	Utah	OL	1968
5. **Larry DeGraw**	Utah	DB	1968-70
6. **Ray Elgaard**	Utah	SB	1983-96
7. **Lee Grosscup**	Utah	QB	1963
8. **L. Rocky Henry**	Utah	WR	2001-03
9. **Airabin Justin**	Utah	CB	2007-08
10. **Doug Kaufusi**	Utah	OL	2005
11. **Gary Kerl**	Utah	LB	1971
12. **Wayne Lammle**	Utah	P	1998-99
13. **Gene LaRocque**	Utah	DT	1981
14. **Curtis Marsh**	Utah	WR	2000-01
15. **Steve Molnar Jr.**	Utah	FB	1969-78
16. **Dale Nosworthy**	Utah	TE	1971
17. **Louie Sakoda**	Utah	P/K	2009-
18. **Mac Speedie**	Utah	WR	1953-54
19. **Bob Pritchett**	Utah	DL	1973

9 Stadiums the Riders Won't Play in Again

Mosaic Stadium/Taylor Field has been around for a century, but here are nine other stadiums that are no longer around in which the Riders have played in at least once...

1. **The Autostade, Montreal**
   Olympic Stadium isn't Montreal's only sports facility mistake! Designed for Expo '67, The Autostade was the home of the Montreal Alouettes from 1968-1976, except for 1972 when the team returned to its previous home Molson Stadium (where it now again plays). The Autostade required renovations almost immediately to fill in the gaps between its seating sections before housing the Alouettes. The 33,000 seat facility was rarely full due to its out of the way and chilly location on the banks of the St. Lawrence. The Riders lost 29-11 to Ottawa in the 1969 Grey Cup there before a capacity crowd of 33,172. The Autostade was demolished shortly after the Alouettes moved to the Big 'O' (Olympic Stadium) in 1977.
2. **Clarke Stadium, Edmonton**
   Before Commonwealth Stadium was built in 1978, the Eskimos played at Clarke Stadium. Built in 1938, it could hold 20,000 spectators for football games. The stadium was demolished in 2000, but the field remains with bleacher seating for around 1,300, and it hosts university and minor sports and other events.
3. **Dominion Park, Regina**
   Essentially the Riders first home field, Dominion Park had grandstand seating for about 600 and was located between 6th and 7th Avenues from Rose to Broad Street, in what is now Regina's Warehouse District. The Riders played here until 1917 when the city sold the site to the T. Eaton Company, which would eventually build the Eaton-Dominion Mall on the site. The mall still stands and currently houses a Sears Outlet Store, Value Village, and several other shops and services.

4. **Empire Stadium, Vancouver**
Built for the 1954 British Empire (Commonwealth) Games, it was the site of the 'Miracle Mile' (record breaking one-mile running race), later in the summer Elvis Presley held his last concert in Canada there, and of course it was where the Riders won their first Grey Cup. The 32,000 seat Empire Stadium housed the BC Lions from their inception in 1954 to 1982, when the club moved to BC Place. The stadium, featuring two grandstands that covered 10,000 of the seats, was demolished in 1993 and the site was a parking lot for Vancouver's fairgrounds, before becoming a soccer field and running track. Ironically, the site will again be the home of the Lions for the 2010 and 2011 seasons with a 27,500 seat temporary stadium called Empire Fields. The temporary stadium is required because BC Place, the Lions' permanent home, is being renovated and fitted with a retractable roof (costing over $450 million, including over $14 million for the temporary stadium – *we're not kidding!*).

5. **Exhibition Park, Regina**
After Dominion Park was sold to Eaton's, the Riders played and practiced at Regina's Exhibition Park grandstand, as well as at Park Hughes and Park de Young (both of which were located on the site of modern day Mosaic Stadium/Taylor Field). The grandstand could seat upwards of 5,000, and even after Parks Hughes and de Young were reconfigured in 1927 to better accommodate the Riders' crowds, the team practiced and had its dressing rooms at Exhibition Park. The grandstand was demolished in 1987 as part of the Queensbury Centre development, and Regina's exhibition grounds and facilities are now known collectively as Evraz Place.

6. **Exhibition Stadium, Toronto**
Also known as CNE Stadium for the Canadian National Exhibition grounds on which it was located, Exhibition Stadium was the home of the Argonauts from 1959 to 1988, after which they moved to the Skydome/Rogers Centre. The stadium sat 33,000 for football when the Argos first played there and 55,000 after it was expanded in 1976 in the hopes of attracting a major league baseball team (the Blue Jays were awarded to Toronto in 1977). The Riders lost the 1976 Grey Cup by three points to Ottawa at Exhibition Stadium. The stadium was demolished in 1999 and is now a soccer stadium - BMO Field, home to the Toronto FC soccer team.

7. **Memorial Stadium, Baltimore**
Built in 1950, Memorial Stadium was home field for the Baltimore Stallions' two CFL seasons in 1994 and 1995, and was notable for actually having a playing surface large enough to accommodate a regulation size CFL field. Seating over 60,000 for football, it had been home to the Baltimore Colts of the NFL until they moved to Indianapolis in 1984 and baseball's Baltimore Orioles until they moved to Camden Yards in 1992. The Riders played there once, on Saturday, October 7, 1995, and squandered a 17-0 lead to lose 29-27 before 31,421 fans. When the NFL returned to Baltimore in 1996, the Ravens played there, but in 1998 they too moved to Camden Yards. Despite spirited efforts to save the venerable old stadium (or parts of it – such as the memorial wall), the stadium was demolished over the course of 2001-02.

8. **Mewata Stadium, Calgary**
Before McMahon Stadium was built in 1959, Calgary football teams played at Mewata Stadium from 1935 to 1959. The stadium was located next to the Mewata Armory at the west end of downtown Calgary. The team's first official game as the 'Stampeders' was at Mewata against the Regina Roughriders on October 22, 1945 (Calgary won 12-0 before 4,000 fans). The stadium was demolished in 1999, and is now the site of the Shaw Millennium skateboard park.

9. **Osborne Stadium, Winnipeg**
Osborne Stadium was the Bombers' home from 1935 until they moved in 1953 to Winnipeg Stadium (now Canad Inns Stadium). The stadium was located in the shadow of the Manitoba Legislative Building and could hold almost 8,000 fans. It was demolished shortly after the Bombers moved, and Winnipeg's Great West Life Building now occupies the site on Osborne Street.

8 Long Serving Assistants, Trainers & Equipment Managers

1. **Sandy Archer – 1951-1980**
   Sandy Archer served for 30 years as the Riders' trainer and athletic therapist. He was a founding member of the Canadian Athletic Therapists Association and is a member of its Hall of Fame.

2. **Norm Fong – 1975-2008**
   Norm Fong was the Riders' head equipment manager for 30 seasons starting in 1979, and was an assistant equipment manager from 1975-78. His position tenure is the longest in the CFL.

3. **Ivan Gutfriend – 1981-present**
   Ivan Gutfriend is now in his 30th season as the Riders' head athletic therapist and trainer, and has been with the team since 1978.

4. **Tare Rennebohm (Senior) – 1932-1957**
   Howard "Tare"Rennebohm played tackle for the Riders for 14 seasons starting in 1916 and again from 1919-31. After his playing career he was an assistant coach for a time, and the team's equipment manager for 25 years, placing his association with the Riders at over 40 years. His son Howard "Tare" Rennebohm Jr. played guard for the Riders from 1946-48.

5. **Richie Hall – 1994-2008**
   Richie Hall served 15 seasons as a Rider defensive coach and coordinator before becoming head coach for Edmonton in 2009. He played four seasons (1988-1991) with the Riders as defensive back.

6. **Dale Laird – 1966-1979**
   Dale Laird served as the team's equipment manager for 14 years.

7. **Alex Smith – 1997-present**
   Alex Smith is currently in his 14th season with the Riders as linebackers coach. He was also a guest coach for the Riders for two years prior to his formal coaching career with the Riders.

8. **Ron Estay – 2001-2008**
   Ron Estay spent eight seasons as the Riders' defensive line coach after playing with BC, Edmonton, and the USFL from 1972-1983, and coaching in the U.S. college system. He is now the lineman coach for the Lafayette Wildcatters of the U.S. Southern Indoor Football League.

Out of the Red & Into the Black
13 Rider Marketing Firsts

They say necessity is the mother of invention, and the Riders have needed a number of inventive strategies over the years to fill the seats and raise revenues; some were successful, others not so much - here are a few of them...

1. **$50-$100-$200-$350 Plate Dinner/Rider Sportsman Dinner/Plaza of Honor Dinner**
   The first fundraiser dinner was held in 1953, cost $50/plate, and featured Rider players, coaches and management, as well as a guest speaker unrelated to the Riders. In 1987, the event became linked to the Rider Plaza of Honor recognizing great Rider players, builders, and teams. The cost of a ticket is now $350. The Plaza event has raised almost $6 million for the team.
2. **Rider Pride Day – October 28, 1979**
   The Riders regular season opened with 12 straight losses under rookie head coach Ron Lancaster, and after a last minute 26-25 win over Edmonton at home on Lancaster's birthday, the Riders had one home game left against BC. With the aid of John Robertson, a former Regina sportswriter/broadcaster (then in Winnipeg) who coined the phrase "Rider Pride", the game was designated Rider Pride Day to fill the stands and raise much needed funds for the organization. The phrase resonated with the public and an overflow crowd of 28,012 watched the Riders beat the Lions 26-12. The club finished at 2-14 (and did so again in 1980), but Rider Pride forever became a part of the Rider Nation vocabulary.
3. **Friends of the Riders Touchdown Lottery**
   In 1986, the Rider organization found itself $600,000 in debt so Rider President Tom Shepherd launched the first ever Touchdown Lottery at $100 a ticket with a grand prize of $100,000. The Lottery was and continues to be a huge success, and has generated over $11 million in net profit to the Club. The 2009 edition awarded a record 1,171 prizes worth $1.6 million.

4. **Tickethon Telethon**
By 1987, years of poor attendance and less than 13,000 in season ticket sales left the Riders almost $2 million in debt. The Riders set a goal of selling 100,000 game tickets and held a 16 hour telethon on June 13th and 14th to help do so. It attracted national media attention and Rider and non-Rider greats answered the phones. In the end, the equivalent of over 77,000 tickets were sold. In 1997 a similar ticket selling ultimatum to sell 200,000 game tickets (or the team would fold), was less well-received and sold 134,000 tickets. Fortunately, the team managed to stay afloat with the help of the ticket sales promotion and the Riders' share of the NFL's $4 million loan to the CFL.

5. **Wrestling, Watkins and Bingo**
In addition to the tickethon telethon noted above, other less enduring fundraising and ticket selling initiatives in 1987 included distributing the Watkins line of products, a province-wide bingo, and staging a World Wrestling Federation (WWF) match prior to the home game on July 4, 1987, against Toronto. Almost 24,000 fans showed up to watch Bret the Hitman Hart, Brutus the Barber Beefcake, and other wrestlers tough it out (and see the Riders and Argos tie at 33-33).

6. **Children's and Teen's Ticket Pricing**
In 1988, the Riders introduced a lower ticket price for children (ages 3-12) and teens (13-18), when accompanied by an adult, allowing them to sit anywhere in the stadium (instead of a specified section).

7. **Pay Per View/Game Broadcasts**
The Riders broadcast their own games a couple of times. The first time was a pay-per-view venture of a 1992 game in Calgary drawing about 2,000 subscribers (the Riders lost 34-30). The second time, involving a 2003 game in BC, was a potential second place/home playoff game showdown and could have lead to a Grey Cup berth (which was in Regina that year); however, because of a gap in the broadcast schedule, the game was not being televised. The Riders responded by having it broadcasted on cable throughout the Province, and won 26-23, but second place and hosting the West Semi-Final went to Winnipeg. The Riders beat Winnipeg (37-21) but lost the West Final to Edmonton who went on to win the Grey Cup against Montreal.

8. **Regina On Board**
Regina On Board is a board game described as a clone of Monopoly, and is based on the city of Regina. Board squares are represented by landmarks and businesses from the Regina area. Proceeds from the game go to benefit the Friends of the Riders through a licensing agreement.

9. **Ownership Shares**
The Riders are one of the last community owned teams in the CFL, and in 2004 became the first CFL team to issue ownership shares as a fundraising and community marketing effort. The limited shares cost $250 ($500 framed), are personalized and numbered, and all 6,000 initial shares were sold by the end of 2008. Rider shareholders get an opportunity to vote on aspects of team leadership and receive other benefits such as discounts on merchandise, seating upgrades, priority parking, and access to special events. For 2010, a 100th anniversary Series II Rider Share is available to commemorate the team's centennial anniversary.

10. **Riderville.com – the Internet & Social Networking**
The Riders embraced the internet and social networking early on as a means of rewarding season ticket and share holders and recruiting new fans. The club's website provides ongoing updates to current and historical team background information along with forums for discussion, debate, and disagreement. Rider fans have returned the embrace partly because there are literally millions of ex-pat Saskatchewanians around the world. In addition to the wealth of content on Riderville.com, the team has more than 34,000 followers on the "Facebook" social networking website, and constant updates on Twitter, which is another online social networking and user messaging service. The Riders also have "The Rider App," a free software application for internet download onto mobile devices. The Rider App provides Rider game statistics and scores, schedules, roster and player information, league results, and news articles and other content in a format easily readable on mobile devices. The Rider App has been downloaded over 11,000 times from over 64 different countries.

11. **The "Store"**

By far the most successful marketing/fundraising initiative is Rider retailing. The Riders were certainly not the first team to merchandise itself, but it is the acknowledged leader among CFL teams. The first permanent store at Taylor Field opened in 1988 and the Riders now have mall stores in each of Regina and Saskatoon, and even opened a temporary store in Calgary during the 2009 Grey Cup. The team reported merchandise sales of over $7 million in 2009. Sales on Labour Day Classic game days alone are in the hundreds of thousands of dollars. It has been reported that of all the merchandise sold every year in the CFL, 40%-50% has a Rider logo.

12. **Licensing Pride**

In May 2010, in honour of the team's 100th anniversary, Saskatchewan Government Insurance (SGI) introduced an official Saskatchewan Roughrider license plate vehicle owners can use and personalize instead of a regular Saskatchewan license plate. The plates feature the team logo and the phrase "Pride Lives Here." Affinity plates for university, college and pro sports teams exist in the US, but the Riders are once again first in the CFL in this regard. By the way, within the first week of availability, over 3,500 plates were ordered.

13. **Guerilla Marketing – Rider Style**

"We Walk Among You", "Hey Eskies fans! We'll save a section for you!" and ads heralding the next meeting of the Rider Nation (away games) are but a few of the billboards placed in opposing team's cities – particularly Calgary, Edmonton, and Winnipeg to reinforce the Rider brand and acknowledge the legions of Rider fans who travel or live across Canada. The Riders' unique marketing is present inside Saskatchewan too, with the latest (and perhaps greatest) being two 20-storey logos, one retro and one current, emblazoned on the Hill Centre Twin Towers in Downtown Regina to celebrate the team's 100th anniversary in 2010.

New Digs for the Riders? By the Numbers

On March 1, 2010, the Riders, along with the City of Regina, and the provincial and federal governments, released a feasibility study into building a new multi-purpose entertainment facility.

Here are a few numbers from the study's various technical reports.

1 = size, in millions of square feet, of proposed facility.

1.1 = estimated operating profit (millions of dollars) of facility based on 31 events (11 Rider games).

3 = pedestrian overpasses/underpasses proposed between the facility and downtown Regina.

3.7 = estimated net income potential (millions of dollars) for the Riders' first season at the facility.

4 = proposed number of levels and number of passenger elevators.

6 = panels comprising retractable roof option.

8 = number of showers in the visiting team dressing room.

12 = number of showers in the home team dressing room.

19 = minimum chair width (in inches).

20 = number of ticket windows.

24 = maximum number of seats between aisles.

25 = feet below grade of playing field.

30 = acres comprising CP Rail's intermodal operations – the site of the proposed facility.

36 = estimated number of months to construct the new facility.

40 = number of private suites.

45 = cost in millions, of the retractable roof option.

46 = overall height (in metres) of proposed facility (125 feet).

75 = press box capacity (written media only - television and radio would be in separate rooms).

194 = estimated volume of wastewater (in cubic metres) during a Rider half-time at new facility.

386 = cost in millions, of the facility, without a retractable roof

431 = cost in millions, of proposed facility, with retractable roof.

525 = proposed restaurant capacity (seating and standing).

639 = number of toilets and urinals for seating capacity of 33,000.

1,000 = distance in metres between Mosaic Stadium and site of proposed new facility.

2,000 = club seating capacity in lower bowl.

2,587 = estimated person years of construction employment impact.

33,000 = seating capacity for football (expandable to 45,000).

53,000 = total potential capacity for concert events.

Source: Saskatchewan Multi-Purpose Entertainment Facility Feasibility Study found at: http://www.cicorp.sk.ca

III. The Fifth Quarter: Awards, Honours & Life Beyond Football

Most Outstanding Riders

West Division:

The Jeff Nicklin Memorial Trophy is presented to the West Division nominee for the CFL's Most Outstanding Player (MOP) Award.

The winner of the award is chosen by voting conducted by the Football Reporters of Canada (FRC) and all CFL head coaches.

Jeff Nicklin was well known across Canada for his athletic endeavours. Born in Fort William, Ontario, Nicklin moved to Winnipeg as a young boy, and went on to excel in various sports, eventually joining the Winnipeg Blue Bombers.

Here are the Riders who've won the Jeff Nicklin Trophy.

Year	Name, Position, Rider Years
2007	**Kerry Joseph,** Quarterback, 2006-07
2005	**Corey Holmes,** Running Back, 2001-05, 2007
1996	**Robert Mimbs,** Running Back, 1995-97
1976	**Ron Lancaster,** Quarterback, 1963-78
1970	**Ron Lancaster,** Quarterback, 1963-78
1966	**Ron Lancaster,** Quarterback, 1963-78
1965	**George Reed,** Running Back, 1963-75
1955	**Ken Carpenter,** Running Back, 1954-59
1951	**Glenn Dobbs,** Quarterback/Punter, 1951-53

CFL:

The CFL's Most Outstanding Player (MOP) Award was established in 1953 (sponsored by Schenley's until 1988) and is annually rewarded to the best player in the CFL.

This is the last award given during the annual CFL Awards banquet, which takes place the week before Grey Cup weekend in the game's host city. The winner of the award is again chosen by vote of the Football Reporters of Canada (FRC) and all CFL head coaches.

The two nominees for the award are the Terry Evanshen Trophy winner from the East Division, and the Jeff Nicklin Memorial Trophy winner from the West Division.

Here are the Riders that went on to be named the CFL's MOP.

Year	Name, Position, Stats (for the season)
2007	**Kerry Joseph**, Quarterback 267 of 459 passes (58.2%); 4,002 yards; 24 TDs; 90 carries for 737 yards and 13 TDs
1976	**Ron Lancaster,** Quarterback 297 of 494 passes (60.1%); 3,869 yards; 25 TDs; 5 carries for 5 yds and 2 TDs
1970	**Ron Lancaster**, Quarterback 175 of 330 passes (53.0%); 2,779 yards; 16 TDs; 21 carries for 71 yds and 2 TDs
1965	**George Reed**, Running Back 274 carries for 1,765 yards (6.4 avg.); 12 TDs 18 receptions for 229 yards; 0 TDs 10 kickoff returns for 225 yards; 0 TDs

16 Things You Might Not Know About "Piffles" Taylor

We all know he's the namesake of Taylor Field, but here are a few things you may not know about Piffles.

1. The N.J. stands for Neil Joseph; 'Piffles' is an expletive he used.
2. He was born in Collingwood, Ontario in 1893, raised in Yellow Grass, Saskatchewan, and died in Regina in 1946.
3. He first played football while at law school at the University of Toronto.
4. He started his playing days with Regina Rugby Club in 1914.
5. He joined the Royal Flying Corps (RFC) in 1916 and was a fighter pilot in World War I.
6. He was shot down in 1917, lost an eye, and spent a year in a prisoner of war camp.
7. His brother Sam, also a RFC fighter pilot, was part of the squadron that shot down the 'Red Baron'. Sam was fatally shot down in 1918.
8. In 1919, Taylor returned to play quarterback for the Riders despite the loss of one eye. Legend has it he lost his glass eye during a game, play stopped until it was found, and then Taylor continued to play.
9. He studied law at the University of Toronto, but never practised it.
10. After his playing days, he was president of the Riders, the Western Inter-provincial Football Union, and the Canadian Rugby Union.
11. He married Mabel Broder of Regina, and helped manage the Broder Financial Agency and the Drake Hotel.
12. He was elected to Regina City Council from 1924 to 1929.
13. He is a charter member of the Canadian Football Hall of Fame.
14. A trophy named after him, The N.J. Taylor Trophy was awarded to the West Division Champions from 1948 to 2004.
15. After his death he was awarded the Order of the British Empire for his courage and contributions to the community.
16. Mosaic Stadium's street address in Regina is 1910 Piffles Taylor Way.

13 Riders Who Became Sportscasters

It has been said that announcers, like athletes, are only as good as their most recent performance...here are a few Riders who became sportscasters...

1. **Ron Lancaster**
   After quarterbacking the Riders for 16 seasons and two seasons as head coach, from 1981-90 Lancaster became a colour commentator for the "CFL on CBC". He left in 1991 to become head coach for the Eskimos, and then head coach and general manager of the Tiger-Cats. He was also a colour commentator for Ti-Cat radio when he passed away in 2008.

2. **Leif Pettersen**
   Pettersen was a wide receiver for the Riders from 1974-77 and for Hamilton from 1978-81. After his playing days ended he served as a game analyst for the "CFL on CTV", and on TSN from the network's inception in 1986. Pettersen passed away in 2008.

3. **Glen Suitor**
   Glen Suitor played safety for eleven seasons with the Riders from 1984-94, and for the last few years of his playing career could be heard on local Regina radio stations. From 1995 to the present he has been TSN's CFL game analyst; a role for which in 2006 he and play-by-play announcer Chris Cuthbert won a Gemini Award.

4. **Carm Carteri**
   Carteri played three seasons as linebacker for the Riders in 1979-80 and 1985, and also played with Hamilton and Montreal. Since retiring from professional football he has been the colour commentator for over twenty years for Rider Radio CKRM.

5. **Jack Gotta**
   Jack Gotta, wide receiver for the Riders from 1960-64, was a commentator in 1984 for the "CFL on CTV." He left in 1985 to become head coach of the Riders.

6. **Daved Benefield**
   Benefield played defensive end for the Riders from 2004-05, and in 2007 was a football analyst on the "CFL on CBC", its last season before the exclusive broadcast rights for the CFL moved to TSN beginning with the 2008 CFL season.
7. **James Curry**
   Curry played defensive tackle for the Riders from 1987-89, and from 1993 to 1996 was a colour commentator for the "CFL on CBC.".
8. **Steve Mazurak**
   Mazurak played wide receiver for the Riders from 1973-80, and served as the Executive Director for the CFL Players Association from 1981 to 1985. Mazurak was a colour commentator on Rider Radio, and is now the team's Vice-President of Marketing and Sales, a position he's held since 2005.
9. **Lee Grosscup**
   Lee Grosscup played one game in 1963 as quarterback for the Riders, after previous stints with various NFL/AFL teams. He returned to the United States the following year and played in the other CFL - the Continental Football League, until 1966 when he began a forty year television and radio broadcasting career on NBC, ABC and local radio covering the NFL, college football, and the USFL. Grosscup also became the first "Voice of the Gold Miners" play-by-play analyst for the short-lived Sacramento Gold Miners, as part of the failed CFL expansion into the U.S.
10. **Bob Brodhead**
    Brodhead was on the 1959 Rider roster as quarterback and also played with Edmonton before returning to the U.S in 1961 to play in the Continental and United leagues. After managing in the NFL with Cleveland, Miami, and Houston, he was the athletic director at Louisiana State University (LSU) and was fired over ethical issues. He wrote a controversial book (*Sacked: The Dark Side of Sports at LSU)* and became a radio personality in Louisiana.

11. **Glenn Kulka**
Kulka was a defensive tackle for the Riders in 1995 and 1996. Prior to the Riders he played with Montreal, Toronto, and Ottawa. After football he became a professional wrestler; at one point he was briefly employed by the WWF (World Wrestling Federation). After his wrestling career, Kulka was as a sports radio talk show host in Ottawa, and provided on-field commentary for Ottawa Renegade football games.

12. **Jack Hartman**
Hartman was a quarterback on the 1950 Rider squad, but is better known as a college basketball coach from 1962 to 1970 for Southern Illinois, and Kansas State University from 1970 to 1986, after which he was colour commentator for college basketball on Manhattan, Kansas, television. He died in 1998.

13. **Glenn Dobbs**
After four seasons (1946-49) playing in the NFL with Los Angeles and Brooklyn, Glenn Dobbs became a sports director for a Tulsa, Oklahoma radio station broadcasting Oklahoma State football games in 1950. It was there that he was approached by members of the Rider executive to play QB for the Riders . . . and the rest is Dobberville history. Dobbs played for the Riders from 1951-53, fast becoming one of the team's most popular players, and was the Riders' head coach in 1952.

A number of other former Rider players have been, or are currently featured as guest analysts on local radio and television sports programs and segments that profile the Riders during football season. The more recent of these guest analysts include:
Greg Fieger, Ron Cherkas, Marshall Hamilton, Bob Poley,
Mike Abou-Mechrek, and Matt Dominguez.

11 Riders in Politics

They say politics is a blood sport...and here are eleven Riders elected to public office...

1. **Robert Leith "Dinny" Hanbidge** (Tackle, 1910-14)
   In 1920, Hanbidge was elected councillor and later Mayor of the Town of Kerrobert, Sask. In 1929, he was elected to the Legislative Assembly of Saskatchewan, serving in Anderson government. He would later go on to be twice elected as a Canadian Member of Parliament. Following his political career in 1963, he was appointed Lieutenant Governor of Saskatchewan, a post he held until 1970.
2. **Galen Wahlmeier** (C/LS/LB, 1957, 1959-63, 1965-67)
   Mayor of Estevan, Sask. (1976-1982)
3. **Corey Holmes** (Running Back, 2001-05, 2007)
   Mayor of Metcalfe, Mississippi (2009-)
4. **Chris Szarka** (Full Back, 1997-)
   Councillor, Ward 10, City of Regina, Sask. (2009-)
5. **Rob Bresciani** (Slot Back, 1988-89)
   Trustee and Chairman, Catholic School Board, Regina, Sask. (1996-)
6. **Neil J. "Piffles" Taylor** (QB, 1914-15, 1919; Exec. 1926-36)
   Councillor, City of Regina, Sask. (1924-1929)
7. **Dale West** (Defensive Back, 1962-68)
   Trustee and Vice-Chair, Board of Education, Regina, Sask. (2006-)
8. **Bruce Cowie** (President, 1976-78)
   Councillor, City of Regina, Sask. (1964-65, 1966-67)
9. **Fred W. Ritter** (Tackle, 1910, Head Coach, 1910-13)
   Councillor, City of Regina, Sask. (1915).
10. **James W. "Jimmy" Kynes** (Centre, 1950)
    Kynes became the youngest Attorney General for the U.S. State of Florida in 1964-65. The Florida Attorney General is an elected cabinet official, serving as the chief legal officer of the state.
11. **Barrin Simpson** (Linebacker, 2010-)
    Okay, maybe he's not an <u>elected</u> official, but Simpson is nicknamed "The Minister of Defense" in recognition of his other job as an ordained minister. Who knows what the future may hold?

Where Are They Now? 21 Interesting Rider Alumni Factoids

In no particular order, here is a random sampling of 21 interesting facts on 22 Rider alumni regarding what they've been up to or where they are...

1. **Lubo Zizakovic** (Defensive Tackle, 1995) is Managing Director, Investment Banking, Lytton Financial, Toronto, Ontario.
2. **Rob Crifo** (Slotback, 1994) is President, Superior Laminated Inc., Concord, Ontario.
3. **Lawrie Skolrood** (Tight End/Offensive Tackle, 1974, 1979-87) is the Deputy Fire Chief, City of Vernon, British Columbia.
4. **Chris Munford** (Defensive Back, 1993) was the Strength and Conditioning Coach for the Charlotte Bobcats of the NBA (National Basketball Association).
5. **Dr. Derek Krete** (Linebacker, 2000) is a sports medicine and rehabilitation specialist in Ontario.
6. **Todd McMillon** (Cornerback, 1997-99) went on the play in the NFL with the Chicago Bears. McMillon lives in Phoenix, Arizona, and is involved with Camp Blitz, billed as Arizona's Premier Youth Football Camps.
7. **Ken Moore** (Tight End/Running Back/Offensive Lineman, 1985-90) created a business along with some colleagues called TENET Medical Engineering, a designer and manufacturer of surgical equipment. TENET's products help surgeons to precisely position and hold limbs in positions that give them the best access and exposure for joint surgery.
8. **Ray Elgaard** (Slotback, 1983-96) is a financial planner with his own business in the United States called Hall of Fame Financial Strategies.

9. **Jeff Fairholm** (Slotback, 1988-93) participates in operating a business called ROI Resources providing products and services for custom designed corporate, industrial and other spaces and control rooms.

10. **Vince Goldsmith** (DE/Linebacker, 1981-83, 1988-90) is the Health Services Manager at the Pierce County Detention and Correction Centre in Tacoma, Washington.

11. **Steve Sarkisian** (Quarterback, 1997-99) has coached in the U.S. college ranks for several years, and in 2009 became the head coach of the University of Washington Huskies.

12. **Joey Walters** (Wide Receiver, 1977-82) is employed by Florida Citrus Sports (FCS) in Orlando. FCS is a non-profit membership organization that promotes civic pride, tourism, economic development, and benefiting charities, educational institutions and the quality of life in the area. A few of the organization's signature events are: The Capital One Bowl, the Champs Sports Bowl, and the Orlando Citrus Parade.

13. **Jim McKean** (Defensive Back/Punter, 1966) also played for the Montreal Alouettes, and went on to become an umpire in Major League Baseball from 1973-2002. He was involved with the MLB up until the spring of 2010.

14. **Tom Clements** (Quarterback, 1979) had a 12 year career in the CFL (Ottawa, Saskatchewan, Hamilton, Winnipeg). During his playing days he completed a law degree and went on to practice law in Chicago from 1988-92. Following his law career, while coaching at Notre Dame he was also an Adjunct Associate Professor at the Notre Dame School of Law where he taught "Sport and the Law." He has been coaching in the NFL since 1992 and is the Quarterbacks coach of the Green Bay Packers.

15. **Ryan Carey** (Safety/Defensive Back 1996-98) played six years in the CFL with Winnipeg and Saskatchewan. After retiring from the CFL he coached at Acadia University and minor football in Ottawa, before joining the military and serving in combat operations in Afghanistan as an Infantry Officer. At one time Carey worked at Canadian Forces Leadership and Recruit School (CFLRS) in St. Jean, Québec, as the Subject Matter Expert (SME) for Leadership.

16. **Bubba Wyche** (Quarterback, 1969, 1971-72) is the owner of a business called The Uptown Greenery Inc. in Atlanta, Georgia.

17. **Daric Zeno** (Wide Receiver, 1985-86) is a teacher and coach at Willowridge High School in Houston Texas. He teaches Health Education and Physical Education.

18. **David Syme** Q.C. (Quarterback, 1976) is a lawyer with the firm Cleall Barristers and Solicitors in Edmonton, Alberta.

19. **Jack Hirose** (Defensive Back, 1980) is a Vancouver-based counselor and training coordinator. Hirose operates a business called Jack Hirose & Associates Inc., offering workshops in mental health, education, and personal growth.

20. **Stacey Hairston** (Defensive Back, 1990-92) is the Defensive Backs coach for the Edmonton Eskimos.

21. **Roger Aldag** (Centre/Guard, 1976-92) and **Bob Poley** (Centre/Tackle/Guard, 1978-84, 1988-92) are both avid fishermen and have an online section on Tourism Saskatchewan's fishing website (www.fishing-in-saskatchewan.com) called "The Tackle Box." The two Saskatchewan-born, former offensive linemen share their fishing memories and opinions, answer questions, and provide fishing tips on a regular basis.

12 Awards & Trophies Inspired By/Named After Riders

1. **N.J. Taylor Trophy** (CFL)
   Named after Neil Joseph 'Piffles' Taylor - WWI fighter pilot, Rider player and president, president of the western and Canadian football unions, and Taylor Field's namesake. Taylor died in 1946, and in 1948 the N.J. Taylor Trophy was awarded to the West Division champions (replacing the Hugo Ross Trophy). The trophy was retired in 2004. The Riders won it eight times.
2. **Dr. Beattie Martin Trophy** (CFL)
   Named after former Riders president Beattie Martin, from 1949 to 1973 this trophy went to the West Division's Most Outstanding Rookie (now the Jackie Parker Trophy). Since 1974, the Dr. Beattie Martin Trophy goes to the West Division's Most Outstanding Canadian. Before being repurposed in 1974, three Riders had won it: Gordon Sturtridge, Harry Lunn, and Lorne Richardson. Since 1974, the Riders' Ray Elgaard, Jeff Fairholm, and Chris Szarka have won it (Elgaard three times).
3. **The DeMarco-Becket Memorial Trophy** (CFL)
   Mel Becket and Mario DeMarco were Rider linemen who died on December 9, 1956 (along with Riders Gordon Sturtridge and Ray Syrnyk, and Bomber Calvin Jones), returning from the All Star Game in Vancouver, when their flight crashed in the Rockies killing all 62 passengers and crew. The families of Becket and DeMarco donated this trophy in 1957 and it was originally given to the West Division Most Outstanding Defensive Lineman. Since 1974, the trophy has been given to the West's Most Outstanding Offensive Lineman. Rider Vic Stevenson won the award once, while Ed McQuarters, Roger Aldag and Andrew Greene each won it twice, and Gene Makowsky has won it three times.
4. **Gord Barwell Award** (CFL)
   Gord Barwell was a star Rider receiver from 1964-73 (one of the Riders top ten all-time in receiving yards and touchdowns). He also helped establish Athletes in Action throughout the CFL, which continues to provide a spiritual chaplain to each CFL team. The Gord Barwell Award is presented each year to a CFL player who exhibits exemplary Christian conduct and leadership on and off the field. Danny Barrett won this award, as did Kerry Joseph.

5. **Eddie James Memorial Trophy** (CFL)
Eddie "Dynamite" James was a star halfback with the Riders in 1928-29, and again in 1931, helping them win the West Championship in all of those years. He then played with Winnipeg and helped them become the first ever western team to win the Grey Cup in 1935. The Eddie James Memorial Trophy has been awarded annually since 1950 to the leading rusher in the West Division. George Reed won the award five consecutive years from 1965 to 1969 and again in 1974. Mike Strickland in 1978, and Robert Mimbs in 1996, are the only other Riders to have won the award.

6. **Ray Syrnyk Memorial Trophy** (Junior Football)
Before Ray Syrnyk played guard for the Riders, he was a Saskatoon Hilltop and captained the Hilltops to their first Canadian Junior Football Championship on home field in 1953. The Ray Syrnyk Memorial Trophy is presented annually by the Hilltops. Syrnyk, along with Riders Mel Becket, Mario DeMarco and Gordon Sturtridge died in a plane crash on December 9, 1956, returning from the East-West All Star Game in Vancouver.

7. **Heinie Rogers Memorial Trophy** (Western Canada Baseball)
Heinie Rogers played for the Riders from 1912-16 and 1920-23, and was the team's head coach in 1916 and 1925. He was also involved in early amateur and semi-pro baseball in Western Canada. The Heinie Rogers Memorial Trophy was awarded by team managers to the most valuable player in the Southern League of the Western Canada Baseball League. Like the Riders, organized baseball in Saskatchewan has a hundred years of history, and early teams included the Regina Bone Pilers, Saskatoon Berry Pickers, and Moose Jaw Robin Hoods. Later Southern League teams included the Regina Red Sox, Swift Current Indians, Moose Jaw Regals, Yorkton Elks, and Melville Millionaires.

8. **The Abbott Cup** (Western Canadian Tier II Junior Hockey)
E.L. "Hickory" Abbott played for the Riders from 1912-15, and was head coach in 1915. He was also a noted hockey player in Western Canada, captaining the Regina Victorias to Junior Championships in 1913 and 1914. He died in active service in WW I, and the Abbott Cup was awarded annually from 1919 through 1999 to the Junior "A" and later Tier II ice hockey champions for Western Canada. The trophy was retired in 1999.

9. **The Hanbidge Cup** (Saskatchewan Tier II Junior A Hockey)
Robert Leith "Dinny" Hanbidge played tackle from 1910-14 for the Regina Rugby Club, and then served in various elected offices including the Saskatchewan Legislative Assembly, Member of Parliament, and Lieutenant Governor of Saskatchewan from 1963-70. Since 1949, the Hanbidge Cup has been presented annually to the provincial Tier II Junior A hockey championship team.

10. **James W. Kynes Award** (Southeastern Conference Football SEC-NCAA)
James W. "Jimmy" Kynes played Centre for the Riders in 1950, and was a star lineman and captain of the University of Florida football team in 1949, playing every minute of every game for the Gators that year. He became the Attorney General for the U.S. State of Florida in 1964-65, and died in 1998 of cancer. The award in his name is presented annually to the offensive lineman who best exemplifies the mental and physical toughness and "iron-man" determination Kynes exhibited as a Gator. Kynes also has a memorial scholarship in his name at the University of Florida.

11. **Leonard Wilson Award** (Purdue University Football)
Len Wilson played halfback for the Riders in 1960, and was a star defensive back and running back from 1957-59 for the Purdue University Boilermakers. Wilson was killed in 1967 in an accident while on duty with the U.S. Armed Forces. Each year Purdue awards a trophy in his honour to the most unselfish and dedicated football player.

12. **The Tom Pate Memorial Award** (CFL)
Tom Pate never played a game for the Riders, but newspaper accounts indicate he was released by the Riders before playing for Hamilton in 1975. Pate, 23, was a rookie linebacker with the Tiger-Cats when during an October 1975 game against Calgary he suffered a head injury (aneurysm). Two days later he died as a result of the injury. The Tom Pate Memorial Trophy is presented by the CFL Players Association (CFLPA) and has been awarded since 1976 to players for outstanding contributions to the league, their team, the association, and the community. Six Riders have won the award: George Reed, Ron Lancaster, Ken McEachern, Jerry Friesen, Richie Hall, and Jeremy O'Day.

Lingerie & Other Football Riders' Alumni Who Coached

Many Rider alumni went on to contribute back to the game they love by coaching other football players in other, and sometimes lesser known, leagues at various levels. Here are 31 Rider alumni who coached or are currently coaching.

Former Rider players who went on to coach in the pros, like Hugh Campbell, Ron Lancaster, Richie Hall and Kent Austin, are profiled in other lists in this book.

1. **Jack Abendschan** (Guard/Placekicker 1965-75) was offensive line and tight end coach at McMurry University in Texas in 2005.
2. **Johnny Babineau** (Guard, 1946) coached the Saskatoon Hilltops from 1947-59, first as an assistant and later as the head coach. Babineau joined Lindsay Holt to be the first coaches of today's Hilltop organization.
3. **Bruce Bennett** (Defensive Back, 1966-72) coached football at Lake Wales High School in Lake Wales, Florida, as part of the Florida High School Athletics Association.
4. **Ryan Carey** (Safety/Defensive Back, 1996-98) coached at Acadia University located in Wolfville, Nova Scotia, and minor football in Ottawa.
5. **Ron Cherkas** (Defensive Tackle, 1976-80, 1982, 1985) is the head coach, special teams coordinator and offensive line coach of the Tartans football program at Campbell Collegiate (high school) in Regina, Saskatchewan. Cherkas was an assistant coach with the Riders in 1989.
6. **Norm Chow** (Guard, 1968) had his career cut short by a knee injury. He has enjoyed a long coaching career in the United States in both the college and National Football League ranks. Chow has been referred to as one of the top offensive coaches in football history, and in 2008 joined the University of California Los Angeles (UCLA) Bruin's as the offensive coordinator and quarterback coach. Earlier in his career, as an offsensive coordinator at Brigham Young University, Chow coached future Rider QB Steve Sarkisian.

7. **Tom Clements** (Quarterback, 1989) has enjoyed a long coaching career in the United States university and National Football League ranks. Clements is currently the quarterbacks coach for the Green Bay Packers of the NFL.
8. **Matt Dominguez** (Wide Receiver, 2003-08) has been coaching with the Riffel Royals of Michael A. Riffel High School in Regina, Saskatchewan. He has also been hosting an annual football camp for several years, serving as the camp head coach, along with other CFL players such as Reggie Hunt, Marcus Adams, Jeremy O'day, Gene Makowsky, Jason Clermont, Wes Cates, and Paul Woldu.
9. **Jason Franci** (Wide Receiver, 1967-68) has coached football at Montgomery High School in Santa Rosa, California, since 1971. Prior to joining the Riders, Franci played in 1966 for the Denver Broncos.
10. **Jerry Friesen** (Linebacker, 1981-86) coached with the Riders in 1996, and in 2001 became the head coach of the University of Alberta Golden Bears where he continues in 2010.
11. **Ralph Galloway** (Offensive Tackle/Guard, 1969-79) spent many years assisting to coach in the football program at Kentwood High School in Covington, Washington, where he is on the teaching staff in Physical Education. Galloway has also coached in the Auburn Junior Football Association in Auburn, Washington.
12. **Art Haege** (Linebacker, 1963) coached 40+ years in the United States at the high school and college levels. Haege also coached in the Arena Football League.
13. **William "Bill" Henry** (Guard, 1988-89) in 2009 was involved with the Big Kahuna South Surrey Rams in the British Columbia Football Conference of the Canadian Junior Football League.
14. **Tom Higgins** (Linebacker, 1980) coached at the college and CFL level (Edmonton and Calgary). Since 2008 he has been the CFL's Director of Officiating.
15. **Lindsay Holt** (Head Coach, 1945, Halfback, 1946) went on in 1947 to serve as the first head coach of the modern-era Saskatoon Hilltops of the Prairie Football Conference.
16. **John Hufnagel** (Quarterback, 1980-83, 1987) began his coaching career as a player/coach with the Riders in 1987. Hufnagel coached in the Arena Football League, the National Football League, and since 2008 has been the head coach and general manager of the Calgary Stampeders.

17. **Dan Johnston** (Slotback/Safety, 1993) was the receivers coach of the Campbell Collegiate Tartans in Regina, Saskatchewan in 2009. Johnston has also coached at camps for the University of Regina Rams and in the Regina Minor Football league.

18. **Robert "Bobby" Jurasin** (Defensive End, 1986-97) coached at Northern Michigan University and participated in some guest coaching at the University of Saskatchewan.

19. **John Kropke** (Defensive Tackle, 1997) in 2008 joined the Hamilton Tiger Cats as the defensive ine coach. Kropke also coached in the CFL in Montreal and Winnipeg, and college ranks in the United States.

20. **Mike Loyd** (Quarterback, 1982) coached at the high school and professional ranks in the United States. In 2008, Loyd became the first football coach of the new Ponte Vedra High School, near Jacksonville, Florida. Loyd also coached at the junior college of Northeastern Oklahoma A&M, where he coached former Rider Richard "Mandrell" Dean (WR/KR, 1999), who was shot and killed on January 27, 2007, in Oklahoma City.

21. **LaDouphyous "Sandman" McCalla** (Cornerback, 2000-04) has done some guest coaching in youth football programs in the United States.

22. **Tom MacCallum** (Tackle, 1993-94) coached at the high school and university ranks in Canada, as well as coaching the offensive line with the University of Regina Rams.

23. **Gerry McGrath** (Kicker, 1985-86) has had a long career with the Concordia University Stingers in Montreal, and has been the head coach since 2000.

24. **Travis Moore** (Wide Receiver, 2003-05) joined the BC Lions in 2010 as a Receivers Coach. He had been with the Hamilton Tiger Cats in 2009 as an offensive assistant and running backs coach. Previously Moore had a few guest coach roles with Montreal (2008) and the NFL's New Orleans Saints (2007). He also spent one season in the Arena Football League coaching wide receivers for the New Orleans Voodoo.

25. **Karl Morgan** (Defensive Tackle, 1983) is an assistant coach (defensive coordinator/defensive line) at the University of North Alabama, a position he's held since 2004.

26. **Joe Paopao** (Quarterback, 1984-86) coached in the CFL with Edmonton, Hamilton, BC, Winnipeg, and Ottawa. Paopao also coached in the short-lived and now defunct XFL, and in the Canadian college ranks with the University of Waterloo.

27. **Traco Rachal** (Linebacker/Defensive Back, 2000-01) is the defensive backs coach and organization's vice-president at the Pride N Skills Academy in Los Angeles, California.

28. **Tommy Reamon** (Running Back, 1977) is a faculty member in the Health and Physical Education department and head coach of the football team (the Eagles) at Landstown High School and Technology Academy in Virgina Beach, Virginia, USA. During prior high school coaching stints, Reamon coached Michael Vick (and his younger brother Marcus) and Aaron Brooks, both of whom went on the become quarterbacks in the NFL. Reamon played six games with the Riders in 1977 (rushing 78 times for 411 yards (5.3 yard avg.), longest 61 yards, and three touchdowns). Reamon was drafted by the Pittsburgh Steelers in the 9th round (223rd overall) of the 1974 NFL Draft. He played with the Florida Blazers (1974) and the Jacksonville Express (1975) of the World Football League (after two seasons, 1974-75, the league folded). He went on to play for the NFL's Kansas City Chiefs in 1976.

29. **Martin Ruby** (Tackle, 1951-57) was an assistant coach with the Riders in 1963. Ruby also coached in the college ranks in the United States, notably at one time joining Rider Glenn Dobbs as an assistant coach at the University of Tulsa.

30. **Larry Thompson** (Wide Receiver, 1994-95, 1998) has guest coached with the Winnipeg Blue Bombers. Thompson was the receivers coach in 2006 with the Vancouver Trojans junior football program in the British Columbia Football Conference of the Canadian Junior Football League.

...and last, but not least...

31. **Llewellyn "Yo" Murphy** (Wide Receiver, 2006-07) is the head coach of the Tampa Breeze women's football team of the Lingerie Football League *(we're not kidding . . . !!)*

20 Things You Might Not Know About Glenn Dobbs

Everyone knows *Riderville*, but there was a time when fans dubbed the land of the green and white "*Dobberville.*" Yes, there was another *'ville'*, and it came to be as a result of the impressive and highly popular Glenn Dobbs Jr., import quarterback/punter (1951-53), and head coach (1952).

It has been reported the frenzy was so intense a Regina retailer marketed and sold "Dobber-Jeans" and "Dobber-Shirts", and there were unofficial license plates emblazoned with "Dobberville." Here are twenty things you might not know about Glenn Dobbs.

1. He was born in McKinney, Texas, July 12, 1920, to parents Glenn Dobbs Sr., a grocery story owner, and mother Mary Tennie (McGraw) Dobbs. He grew up in McKinney, Texas, and Frederick, Oklahoma; he graduated high school in Frederick.
2. The greatest athlete to come out of the University of Tulsa, Dobbs played with the Golden Hurricane football team from 1940-43. Dobbs graduated a Dean's Honour Roll student with a Bachelor of Arts degree in 1943. Just a few of his athletic records at the University of Tulsa are:
   - In 1942, he was the punting leader in the USA with a 48.3 yard average;
   - Led his team in passing in 1941-42. In 1942 Dobbs completed 62.6% of his passes, throwing only four interceptions;
   - Led his team in interceptions in 1942 with four;
   - Has the best punting average in a game (in 1942 versus Oklahoma State), with an average punt of 65.2 yards
   - Tied for first-place all-time for an 87 yard punt in 1942;
   - Second place all-time for a 79 yard punt in 1940;
   - Fourth place all-time for a 78 yard punt in 1942;
   - Fifth place all-time for a 77 yard punt in 1940;
   - Eighth place in all-time pass efficiency with a 138.8 rating in 1942.
3. Dobbs placed 9th in the Heisman Trophy voting race of 1942.

4. The Sun Bowl, played January 1, 1942, in front of 12,000 fans in El Paso, Texas, saw Dobbs punt and pass Tulsa to victory over Texas Tech with a score of 6-0. After half-time, Dobbs punted from his own 14 yard line, sending the ball through the Tech's end zone. Late in the game, Dobbs' passing mounted a 71 yard touchdown drive, and while Dobbs' point after attempt was blocked, Tulsa held on to the lead and won the game.

5. Dobbs (6'4", 211 lbs) was a first round pick (third overall) in 1943 by the Chicago Cardinals of the NFL. The two didn't come to terms and at the age of 22 Dobbs joined the U.S. Army Air Force, eventually becoming a Lieutenant. Dobbs played football for the Air Force team, Randolph Field, and took his team to the 1944 Cotton Bowl Classic playing against the University of Texas. Dobbs and another future Rider, Martin Ruby, played together on the Randolph Field team, and were both given Outstanding Player nods in this bowl game. The game ended in a 7 – 7 tie (see 17 Interesting Individual Rider Firsts).

6. Dobbs' younger brother Bobby was also drafted by the Chicago Cardinals in the 13th round of the 1944 NFL draft; in that same draft, future Rider John Green (DB, 1953) was selected by Philadelphia in the 16th round. Green would go on to play for the Philadelphia Eagles for five seasons (1947-51).

7. In 1946 Dobbs began the first of four seasons (1946-49) playing in the NFL with the Los Angeles Dons and Brooklyn Dodgers.

8. In 1950 Dobbs was lured (reportedly with a $25,000 salary) out of retirement to come up north and play for the Riders. Dobbs played for three seasons (1951-53) and was the Riders' head coach in 1952.

9. Younger brother Bobby Lee Dobbs coached Tulsa from 1955-60, and in 1955, Glenn returned to his alma mater and the position of athletics director (a position he held until 1970). In 1955, Dobbs was an assistant coach to his brother, and they were joined by former Rider Martin Ruby who came to help coach the offensive line. In 1961, Glenn took over the head coaching job from his brother. Glenn coached Tulsa from 1961-68 for a total of 82 games, with a 54.9% win record (45 wins, 37 losses), placing him fifth in the Top 10 winningest coaches for Tulsa. Glenn was the Missouri Valley Conference football Coach of the Year in 1962, an award his brother also received in 1959. In the 1960s Dobbs' Golden Hurricane team changed the U.S. college football landscape with its passing game. Tulsa led the USA in passing for five straight seasons: 1962-66.

10. Glenn's brother Bobby left Tulsa to be head coach of the Calgary Stampeders from 1961-64.

11. Dobbs is in the (USA) College Football Hall of Fame (1980), the University of Tulsa Hall of Fame (1982), the Oklahoma Sports Hall of Fame (1988), and the Riders' Plaza of Honor (1988). Dobbs also received a Pioneer All-America Award from the All-American Football Foundation in 2001.

12. While at the University of Tulsa, Dobbs coached these future Riders:

    - Rick Eber (Wide Receiver, 1973). Eber was second in receiving yards in 1973 for the Riders with 730 yards. Prior to the Riders, Eber played three seasons in the NFL (1968-70), two with San Diego and one with the Atlanta Falcons;
    - Ken Reed (Defensive End/Linebacker, 1965-70). Reed was drafted by San Francisco 49ers in the 17th round of the 1963 NFL draft, though besides the Riders his professional football career only included two seasons with Edmonton (1963-64);
    - Bill Goods (Fullback, 1968). Goods had 22 carries for 98 yards, and 7 receptions for 76 yards in 1968 for the Riders. Goods played in Calgary for two seasons (1965-66) and in Edmonton for one (1969);
    - Henry "Hank" Dorsch (Fullback/Defensive Back, 1964-71). Dorsch, born in Saskatchewan, led the Golden Hurricane in rushing in 1962 and 1963. Dorsch later served as a Rider General Manager in 1978-79; and,
    - Rob Pyne, (Defensive Back, 1972-73). Pyne, another Saskatchewanian, went to Tulsa on a football scholarship and for one season was coached by Dobbs. Pyne also played in Winnipeg (1973-74) and Calgary (1974).

13. The University of Tulsa Golden Hurricane football program retired Dobbs' jersey number 45.

14. Following his coaching and football days, Dobbs worked in public relations and management of a gas and oil distributorship, and was in 1977 the manager of the Tulsa Drillers minor league baseball team.

15. Dobbs coached a semi-pro football team in the United States in the late 1970's. The Tulsa Mustangs played five games of a fifteen-game American Football Association season before disbanding.

16. Dobbs' two sons also played football for Tulsa, and were coached by their father. John Dobbs led the Golden Hurricane in passing in 1970. Glenn Dobbs III (graduated with a B.S. in 1968), also a quarterback with Tulsa in the 1960s, taught school in Tulsa and Florida before returning to Tulsa to work in his dad's (Rider Glenn Dobbs Jr.) oil business in Owasso, Oklahoma. Dobbs III teaches physical science at Union Intermediate High School, Broken Arrow, Oklahoma, having taught for 21 years in the area.

17. There is a fourth generation of Glenn Dobbs – Glenn Dobbs IV, Dobbs' grandson.

18. Dobbs was surprised on his 80th birthday with a lifetime membership in the Tulsa University Lettermen's Association.

19. On October 21, 2000, Glenn Dobbs Drive was unveiled on the University of Tulsa campus, renaming Eighth Street between Harvard and Florence Avenues after Dobbs.

20. Dobbs passed away on the evening of Tuesday, November 12, 2002, at his home in Tulsa, Oklahoma. A memorial service was held Monday, November 18, at 10:00 a.m., at the Donald W. Reynolds Center on the University of Tulsa campus. At the November 16, 2002, Tulsa-San Jose State football game, Tulsa players wore number 45 on their helmets and a moment of silence was held in Dobbs' honour. Also in Dobbs' honour is a Glenn Dobbs Athletic Fund at the Department of Intercollegiate Athletics, University of Tulsa.

25 Popular Rider Players

Since 1979, an award has been presented annually to the most popular Rider as voted by the fans. The award was called the Molson Cup from 1979-2008, and since 2009 is known as the Wireless Age Most Popular Roughrider.

Here are the award winners and the year(s) in which they won it...

1. **Mike Strickland**, Running Back - 1979
2. **Ken McEachern**, Defensive Back/Safety - 1980
3. **Joey Walters**, Wide Receiver - 1981, 1982
4. **Chris DeFrance**, Wide Receiver - 1983, 1984
5. **Eddie Lowe**, Linebacker - 1985
6. **Bobby Johnson**, Running Back - 1986
7. **Bobby Jurasin**, Defensive End - 1987, 1997
8. **Dave Ridgway**, Placekicker - 1988
9. **Tim McCray**, Running Back - 1989
10. **Richie Hall**, Defensive Back - 1990
11. **Willis Jacox**, Wide Receiver/Slotback - 1991
12. **Ray Elgaard**, Slotback - 1992
13. **Jerald Bayliss**, Defensive Tackle - 1993
14. **Donald Narcisse**, Wide Receiver - 1994, 1995, 1998
15. **Robert Mimbs**, Running Back - 1996
16. **Mike Saunders**, Running Back - 1999
17. **Henry Burris**, Quarterback - 2000
18. **Darren Davis**, Running Back - 2001
19. **Chris Szarka**, Fullback - 2002, 2003
20. **Nate Davis**, Defensive Tackle - 2004
21. **Corey Holmes**, Running Back - 2005
22. **Fred Perry**, Defensive End - 2006
23. **Kerry Joseph**, Quarterback - 2007
24. **Weston Dressler**, Wide Receiver - 2008
25. **Darian Durant**, Quarterback - 2009

5 Riders Who Won CFL Coach of the Year

The CFL Coach of the Year is selected by the Football Reporters of Canada (FRC) and is awarded to the coach who most demonstrates exceptional leadership, dedication, and excellence during the regular season. The award is named in honour of Annis Stukus, who head coached for Edmonton and BC and later became a member of the FRC.

Five Rider head coaches have won the award...

1. **Kent Austin – 2007**
   In his first (and so far only) year as Rider head coach, Austin coached the Riders to a 12-6 season, to the West Division championship (the first since 1997), and to the team's third Grey Cup win.
2. **John Gregory – 1989**
   In his third year as Rider head coach, Gregory coached the Riders to a 9-9 season, to the West Division championship (the first since 1976), and to the team's second Grey Cup win.
3. **Joe Faragalli – 1981**
   In his first year as Rider head coach, Faragalli coached the team to an 11-7 season, fourth in the West. It was the team's first winning season in five years and followed two consecutive 2-14 seasons.
4. **Eagle Keys – 1968**
   Keys is sixth all-time among CFL head coaches in seasons coached and regular season wins (with Saskatchewan, BC and Edmonton), but won his only Coach of the Year award in his fourth year as Rider head coach, taking the team to a first place 12-3-1 record in 1968. In his six Rider seasons, Keys coached the team to four first place finishes, four Grey Cup appearances and its first Grey Cup in 1966.
5. **Steve Owen – 1962**
   Legendary NFL (New York Giants) head coach Steve Owen became the Riders' head coach in 1961, inheriting a team that finished well out of the playoffs the two previous seasons with records of 1-15 and 2-12-2. Owen's 1962 Riders finished at 8-7-1, making the western playoffs (losing to Calgary). Owen left the Riders in 1963, and died in 1964. In 1966, he was voted into the Pro Football Hall of Fame.

Tom Pate Memorial Trophy Winners

The Tom Pate Memorial Trophy has been awarded by the CFL Players Association (CFLPA) since 1976 to players who "display qualities that distinguish them from their peers" and for outstanding contributions to the league, their team, the association and the community.

Pate was a 23 year old rookie linebacker with the Hamilton Tiger-Cats (joining the team after being released by the Riders) who suffered a head injury (aneurysm) after delivering a block in the fourth quarter of a game against the Stampeders in October, 1975. He left the game unconscious, and died just two days later.

To date six Riders have won the award...

Year	Name, Position, Rider Years
2008	**Jeremy O'Day,** Guard, 1999-present
1990	**Richie Hall,** Defensive Back, 1988-91
1985	**Jerry Friesen,** Linebacker, 1981-85
1981	**Ken McEachern,** Defensive Back/Safety, 1974-82, 1984
1977	**Ron Lancaster,** Quarterback, 1963-78
1976	**George Reed,** Running Back, 1963-75

Riders & The Heisman Trophy

The Heisman Trophy Trust of New York City awards the annual Heisman Memorial Trophy to an individual voted the most outstanding college football player in the United States. First awarded in 1935, the bronze statue award weighs 45 pounds and depicts a football player side-stepping and straight arming a potential tackler. The trophy is named after John William Heisman, a prominent football player and innovative college football coach and strategist in the United States.

The following list shows Riders who were in the Heisman Trophy voting, listed in alphabetical order...

Name/ Position	Voting Rank	Voting Year	Rider Years
1. **Michael Bishop, QB**	2nd	1998	2008
2. **Tom Clements, QB**	4th	1974	1979
3. **Glenn Dobbs, QB/P**	9th	1942	1951-53
4. **Lee Grosscup, QB**	10th	1957	1963
5. **Graham Harrell, QB**	4th	2008	2009
6. **John Hufnagel, QB**	6th	1972	1980-83, 1987
7. **Larry Isbell, DB/P**	7th	1951	1954-58
8. **Tony Rice, QB**	4th	1989	1990

Note: Quarterback Pat Sullivan won the Heisman Trophy in 1971, and after four seasons with the NFL's Atlanta Falcons (1972-75), joined the Riders in 1977 but never saw any game action. The Regina Leader Post reported Sullivan attended one practice and promptly returned to the United States.

20 Things You Might Not Know About 'Big Al' Benecick

Al Benecick was a Rider offensive lineman (tackle) for ten years, from 1959 to 1968. Here are twenty things you might not know about him...

1. Born Alexander Benecick, March 20, 1937, in Bristol, Connecticut.
2. Al lived at 46 Oak Street (address no longer exists) in the City of Bristol (population 61,353). Located about twenty minutes southwest of Hartford, Bristol is the home of American sports television network ESPN (Entertainment Sports Programming Network).
3. Al, or 'Big Al' as he was known by his Bristol high school teammates, attended Bristol Central High School. He played the violin as a youngster, and initially became interested in football by a few simple hellos from prominent Bristol athletics coach Tom M. Monahan. Being noticed by a prominent and positive community role model had meaning to young Al. Later, Benecick credits Bristol coach Tom R. Monahan Jr. (and his coaching father Tom M. Monahan Sr.) with getting him involved in football.
4. Al attended Syracuse University (located in Syracuse, New York) in 1956, where he would become an All-Time Letterwinner (1956-57-58) and play alongside future U.S. football legend, and actor, Jim Brown. Besides football, Al was also on the 1958 Syracuse wrestling team.
5. The October 8, 1956, edition of *LIFE* magazine, sold for 20 cents. The cover featured a photo of the State Grandmasters who led Freemasonry (the Masons) in the USA. The magazine's sports section featured an article titled "Syracuse Gets Off the Ground – Fit Muscles and a back named Brown help an ambition." The story begins under a large photo with the caption: "Star Syracuse Halfback Jim Brown (left) hangs on in rope-climbing drill, behind are Mike Bill, Ron Luciano, Al Benecick, Frank Manbuca." The article is a brief essay on the Syracuse football team, an underdog, but being readied to punch above its weight with the help of future legend and hall of fame running back Jim Brown.

6. Benecick's college football head coach was Ben Schwartzwalder, who coached at Syracuse from 1949-73. Schwartzwalder was a decorated World War II major and paratrooper, and in 1967 was elected president of the American Football Coaches Association. He would also be inducted into the U.S. College Football Hall of Fame in 1982.

7. With the Syracuse Orangemen, Al played in the 1957 Cotton Bowl Classic (today called AT & T Cotton Bowl Classic). On New Year's Day 1957, Syracuse played against Texas Christian in front of 61,500 fans. Despite legendary running back Jim Brown's performance of rushing for 132 yards, three touchdowns, and kicking three extra points, and no doubt Al's intense play opening holes on the offensive line, Syracuse lost the game 28-27.

8. In Al's final season with Syracuse he went to the Orange Bowl on January 1, 1959 (Miami, Florida), where he was the team's co-captain with Chuck Zimmerman. Syracuse would lose to Oklahoma 21-6.

9. Al was picked in the sixth round (62nd overall) of the 1959 NFL Draft by the Philadelphia Eagles, but failed to make the team. Other 1959 NFL Draft picks who went on to become Riders include:

    - Don Allard (Rider quarterback 1960-61, picked in round one, 4th overall, by the Washington Red Skins);
    - Lee Grosscup (Rider quarterback 1963, picked in round one, 10th overall, by the New York Giants);
    - Bill Butler (Rider defensive back, 1965, picked in round nineteen, 217th overall, by the Green Bay Packers);
    - Bob Ptacek (Rider quarterback and linebacker 1960-65, picked in round eight, 87th overall); and
    - Ferdie Burket (Rider fullback and punter 1959-62, picked round fourteen, 168th overall, by the Baltimore Colts.)

10. After graduating from Syracuse University, and failing to make the Philadelphia Eagles team, Al, known in Rider circles as "Benny," headed up north and joined the Riders in 1959 as an offensive tackle. He would become a dominant force in the CFL, remaining with the Riders through the 1968 season.

11. Benecick wore number 66 while playing with the Riders.

12. While Benecick was with the Riders, two other Syracuse alumni joined the team. Dave Sarette was with the Syracuse Orangemen in the 1959-60-61 seasons, and joined the Riders in 1962 (quarterback). John Paglio was with Syracuse for three seasons, 1961-62-63, and joined the Riders in 1965 (tackle). Each of these Syracuse Riders was coached by Ben Schwartzwalder.

13. For several years during his time with the Riders (1965-69), Al did some coaching and was the assistant athletic director at the University of Saskatchewan Regina Campus (the campus became the University of Regina in 1974). He worked at the university in the morning and attended football practice in the afternoon. It is not uncommon, then, or now, for Riders to have careers outside of football.
14. Benecick played his final season in the CFL with the Edmonton Eskimos in 1969, playing just four games before retiring, as part of the deal to join Edmonton included an opportunity to coach.
15. Following his playing career, Benecick took on the role of offensive line coach for the Eskimos until 1971.
16. Benecick returned to the U.S. and in 1975 was a teacher and offensive line coach under Jim Stutts, the football head coach at the Admiral Farragut Academy. Farragut is a private college preparatory school and Honor Naval Academy on the shores of Boca Ciega Bay in St. Petersburg, Florida.
17. While at Farragut, coach Benecick was joined by former Syracuse teammate Maury Youmans. Youmans had spent five seasons as a defensive end in the NFL; three with the Chicago Bears (1960-62) and two with the Dallas Cowboys (1964-65). Youmans would go on to co-author two football books with his brother Gary: *'59: The Story of the 1959 Syracuse National Championship Football Team*, and *'63: The Story of the 1963 World Championship Chicago Bears*.
18. Al was inducted into the Saskatchewan Roughriders' Plaza of Honor in 1991.
19. Al's football prowess was well regarded across Canada, leading to his induction to the Canadian Football Hall of Fame in 1996, alongside teammate and Rider great Bill Clarke (defensive tackle, 1951-64).
20. In 1996, Al was inducted into the City of Bristol Sports Hall of Fame.

Plaza of Honor*
Who, When, & What Position

You'll see their names in lots of publications, but here is a complete list of who they are, when they were inducted, the position they played, and the years they were a Rider...

Induction Year

2010
- 1966 Grey Cup Winning Team
- 1989 Grey Cup Winning Team
- 2007 Grey Cup Winning Team

2009
- Tom Burgess, Quarterback (1987-89, 1994-95)
- Dan Farthing, Slotback (1991-2001)
- Norm Fong, Equipment Manager (Assistant 1975-1978, Head 1979-2008)

2008
- Tom Campana, Running Back/Slotback (1972-77)
- Ted Provost, Safety (1973-77)
- Lawrie Skolrood, Tight End/OT (1974, 1979-87)

2007
- Steve Dennis, Cornerback (1977-84)
- Vic Stevenson, Offensive Tackle (1983-92, 1998)
- Bobby Thompson, Running Back (1969-74, 1977)

2006
- Rhett Dawson, Receiver (1974-79)
- Gary Lewis, Defensive Tackle (1985-94)
- Ken Reed, Defensive End/Linebacker (1965-70)

2005
- Jeff Fairholm, Slotback (1988-93)
- Tim Roth, Defensive Tackle, (1971-77)
- John Wozniak, Centre/Linebacker (1953-56)

2004
- Steve Mazurak, Wide Receiver (1973-80)
- Mike Anderson, Centre/Guard (1984-95)
- Henry (Hank) Dorsch, Fullback/DB (1964-71), General Manager (1978-79)

2003
- Donald Narcisse, Wide Receiver (1987-99)
- Larry Dumelie, Defensive Back (1960-67)
- John Lipp, President (1993-95)

2002
- Bobby Jurasin, Defensive End (1986-97)
- Larry Bird, Centre (1971-78)
- Gary Brandt, Guard (1967-77)

2001
- John Payne, Head Coach (1973-76)
- Bob Ptacek, Quarterback/Linebacker (1960-65)
- Bill Manchuk, Linebacker (1971-80)
- Doug Killoh, Defensive End (1953-60)

2000
- Bruce Cowie, President (1976-78)
- Cleveland Vann, Linebacker (1976-80)
- Dave Ridgway, Placekicker (1982-95)

1999
- Ray Elgaard, Slotback (1983-96)
- Kent Austin, Quarterback, (1987-93)
- Larry Isbell, Defensive Back/Punter (1954-58)

1998
- Glen Suitor, Safety (1984-94)
- Roger Goree, Linebacker (1975-80)
- Johnny Bell, End (1946-52)

1997
- Bob Kosid, Defensive Back (1964-72)
- Dale West, Defensive Back (1962-68)
- Dick Rendek, Director and President (1982-84)
- Lorne Richardson, Defensive Back (1973-76)

1996
- Bob Poley, Centre/Tackle/Guard (1978-84, 1988-92)
- John Gregory, Head Coach (1987-91)
- Ralph Galloway, Offensive Tackle/Guard (1969-79)
- Jim Worden, Tight End (1964-69)
- Stan Williams, Defensive Back (1953-57)

1995
- Wally Dempsey, Linebacker (1965-69, 1972)
- Tom Shepherd, Director (1980-2005), President (1986-89 "involved" since 1966
- Clyde Brock, Offensive Tackle (1964-75)
- Eddie Lowe, Linebacker (1983-91)
- Gene Wlasiuk, Defensive Back (1959-67)

1994
- Vince Goldsmith, DE/Linebacker (1981-83, 1988-90)
- Wayne Shaw, Linebacker (1961-72)
- Gord Barwell, Wide Receiver (1964-73)

	• Mike Cassidy, Offensive Tackle/Defensive End (1948-55) • Chris DeFrance, Wide Receiver (1981-85)
1993	• Roger Aldag, Centre, Guard (1976-92) • Ken McEachern, Defensive Back (1974-82, 1984) • Ted Dushinski, Defensive Back (1965-75) • Gord Staseson, President (1979-82) • Maurice Williams, Guard (1939-42, 1948) • Neil "Piffles" Taylor, Quarterback (1914-15, 1919), Executive (1926-33), President (1934-36)
1992	• Howie Milne, Player (1920-28), Head Coach (1926-28) • Jack Abendschan, Guard/Placekicker (1965-75) • Neil Habig, Centre (1958-64) • Reg Whitehouse, Offensive Tackle/Guard (1952-66) • Alan Ford, Fullback/Receiver/Punter (1965-76), General Manager (1989-99)
1991	• Howard "Tare" Rennebohm Sr., Guard (1916, 1919-31), Equipment Manager (1932-57) • Johnny Garuik, Offensive Line (1930-43) • Sully Glasser, Fullback/Quarterback (1946-57) • Darrell (Del) Wardien, Halfback/Placekicker (1948-54) • Al Benecick, Offensive Tackle (1959-68) • Bruce Bennett, Defensive Back (1966-72) • William E. Clark, Executive (1961) • Mike Samples, Defensive Tackle (1978-83)
1990	• J. D. "Jack" Rowand, Halfback (1923-24) • S. D. (Stacey Daniel) "Stack" Tibbits, President (1949) • D. S. McDonald, President (1950, 1966-67) • Clarence "Toar" Springstein, Tackle (1939-41, 1946, 1949-52) • Pete Martin, Guard (1946-51) • Garner Ekstran, Defensive End (1961-67) • Joey Walters, Wide Receiver (1977-82) • Bill Baker, Defensive End (1968-73, 1977-78), General Manager (1987-88)
1989	• Ken Carpenter, Running Back (1954-59) • Jack Hill, Running Back/Wide Receiver (1957-61) • Ed McQuarters, Defensive Tackle (1966-74)

- Bobby Marlow, Full Back/Linebacker (1953-60)
- Frank Tripucka, Quarterback (1953-59,1963), HC (1959)
- Al Urness, Lineman (1928-31)
- Ted Urness, Centre/Guard (1961-70)
- Clair Warner, Player (1919, 1924-33), President (1941), GM (1946-49, 1951-52), Executive (1934-70)
- Bob Walker, Lineman (1934-46)

1988

- Sandy Archer, Head Trainer (1951-80)
- Gordon Barber, Lineman, Executive (1929-33)
- Hugh Campbell, Wide Receiver (1963-67,1969)
- Ken Charlton, RB/Punter (1941,1943, 1948-54)
- Bill Clarke, Defensive Tackle (1951-64)
- Glenn Dobbs, Quarterback/Punter (1951-53), HC (1952)
- Greg Grassick, HC/Player (1929,1934), GM (1950)
- Don McPherson, Director (1949-73), President (1956-57)
- Martin Ruby, Tackle (1951-57)

1987

- Ron Lancaster, Quarterback (1963-78), HC (1979-1980)
- George Reed, Running Back (1963-75)
- Fred Wilson, Kicker (1913-32)
- Ron Atchison, Defensive Tackle (1952-68)
- Ken Preston, Quarterback (1940, 1943, 1946-48), Head Coach (1946-47), General Manager (1958-78)
- Dean Griffing, Player/Head Coach (1936-38, 1940-41, 1943), General Manager (1954-57)
- Al Ritchie, Head Coach, (1930-32, 1935, 1942), Manager (1921-24)
- Bob Kramer, President (1951-53, 1961-65)
- Eagle Keys, Head Coach (1965-70), Assistant (1964)

* The spelling of 'honor' using the American spelling (versus the Canadian/British 'honour') is intentional, sort of. Rider sources tell us when the Plaza was first established the American spelling was inadvertently used for printing. Given the team's fortunes at the time, they could not afford to change the materials developed for the event, so the spelling remained. This spelling appears on the Plaza of Honor cairn outside the main gates of Mosaic Stadium.

75th Anniversary Dream Team

For the Riders' 75th anniversary in 1985, the club selected a "Dream Team." Here they are with their Rider years...

Quarterback Ron Lancaster (1963-78)

Running Backs George Reed (1963-75),
Bobby Marlow (1953-60)

Receivers Hugh Campbell (1963-67, 1969)
Rhett Dawson (1974-76)
Joey Walters (1977-82)
Chris DeFrance (1981-85)

Centre Ted Urness (1961-70)

Guards Al Benecick (1959-68),
Jack Abendschan (1965-75)

Offensive Tackles Martin Ruby (1951-57),
Clyde Brock (1964-75)

Defensive Lineman Ron Atchison (1952-68)
Garner Ekstran (1961-67)
Bill Baker (1968-73, 1977-78)
Ed McQuarters (1966-74)

Linebackers Wally Dempsey (1965-69, 1972),
Roger Goree (1975-80)
Wayne Shaw (1961-72)

Defensive Backs Bruce Bennett (1966-72),
Lorne Richardson (1973-76)
Ken McEachern (1974-82, 1984),
Ted Dushinski (1965-75)
Steve Dennis (1977-84)

Placekicker Jack Abendschan (1965-75)
Punter Glenn Dobbs (1951-53)

Head Coach Eagle Keys (1965-70)

General Manager Ken Preston (1958-78)

8 Retired Rider Numbers & Their Stories

You see their names and numbers stretched across the top of the west side grandstand of Mosaic Stadium, and they each appear in more than one of the lists in this book. Here they are with their stories...

1. **#40 Mel Becket**, Centre (1953-56)
2. **#55 Mario DeMarco**, Guard (1953-56)
3. **#56 Ray Syrnyk**, Guard (1954-56)
4. **#73 Gordon Sturtridge**, Defensive End (1953-56)

   Roughriders' Becket, DeMarco, Syrnyk and Sturtridge (and wife) were passengers on Trans-Canada Air Lines Flight 810 on December 9, 1956, with another CFL player, Calvin Jones, of the Winnipeg Blue Bombers. All five players were at the 1956 CFL All-Star game in Vancouver, BC, and were travelling home on Flight 810 when the plane crashed into Mount Slesse. From Vancouver, the flight was to fly on to Calgary, Regina, Winnipeg, Toronto, and Montreal. The five players were accompanied by 54 other passengers, and three crew members, all of whom died. The Roughriders retired the four Riders' jersey numbers shortly after the accident.

5. **#34 George Reed**, Running Back (1963-75)
   Not much needs to be said about George Reed's accomplishments and why his number is retired. He is the Riders' all-time leader in touchdowns, rushing attempts, rushing yards and rushing touchdowns. He is the fourth all-time Rider in points scored (the only non-kicker in the top five) and he continues to hold CFL records for rushing attempts, rushing touchdowns, playoff rushing yards, playoff rushing touchdowns, and the most 1,000 yard rushing seasons (11). He has sixty-six 100-yard rushing games in his career, won the CFL's Most Outstanding Player in 1965, and was a CFL all-star nine times and a western division all-star ten times.

6. **#23 Ron Lancaster**, Quarterback (1963-78), Head Coach (1979-80)
   Not much needs to be said here either; Lancaster is the team's all-time leader in passing attempts, completions, and passing yardage. He is third all-time in games played and second in seasons played. He continues to hold CFL records for playoff passing yards (career and single season), and playoff passing touchdowns (career and single playoff game). He was twice awarded Coach of the Year honours (with Edmonton and Hamilton).

7. **#36 Dave Ridgway**, Placekicker (1982-95)
   Ridgway is the Riders' all-time leader in points, converts (made and attempted) and field goals. He is sixth all-time in games played and tied for fourth place all-time in seasons played. He continues to hold CFL records for most field goals in a regular season and most consecutive field goals in a regular season, and he shares the record for most field goals in a single regular season game and most field goals in one quarter. His memorable kick against Hamilton in 1989 won the Riders' second Grey Cup.

8. **#44 Roger Aldag**, Centre/Guard (1976-92)
   Roger Aldag is the team's all-time leader in games played, and shares with Ron Atchison the record for most seasons played. He is the epitome of the Saskatchewan-born-and-raised hard work ethic. He was a CFL all-star four times and West Division all-star eight times, and named the CFL's Outstanding Offensive Lineman twice. Perhaps more telling is he was voted the most outstanding lineman by his peers four times. He was also one of the team's captains during the 1989 grey Cup winning season.

35 Riders in the Canadian Football Hall of Fame

Here are 35 Riders recognized across the CFL for their achievements on and off the field.

Although most Rider inductees played in the CFL, this list also includes those inducted as builders who served in the Riders' coaching or executive ranks at some point.

Rider Player or Executive	Induction Year & Category	Rider Years
1. **Roger Aldag**	2002, Player	1976-92
2. **Ron Atchison**	1978, Player	1952-68
3. **Bill Baker**	1994, Player	1968-73, 1977-78 (as player)
4. **Greg Battle**	2007, Player	1996
5. **Al Benecick**	1996, Player	1959-68
6. **Hugh Campbell**	2000, Builder	1963-1967, 1969
7. **Ken Charlton**	1992, Player	1941, 1943, 1948-54
8. **Bill Clarke**	1996, Player	1951-64
9. **Tom Clements**	1994, Player	1979
10. **Andrew Currie**	1974, Builder	1928, 1930
11. **Ray Elgaard**	2002, Player	1983-96
12. **Dean Griffing**	1965, Player	1936-41 (as player)
13. **Eddie James**	1963, Player	1928-29, 1931
14. **Gerry James**	1981, Player	1964
15. **Alondra Johnson**	2009, Player	2004
16. **Bobby Jurasin**	2006, Player	1986-97

Rider Player or Executive	Induction Year & Category	Rider Years
17. **Eagle Keys**	1990, Builder	1965-70
18. **Bob Kramer**	1987, Builder	1951-1953, 1961-65
19. **Ron Lancaster**	1982, Player	1963-78 (as player)
20. **Don McPherson**	1983, Builder	1949-1973
21. **Ed McQuarters**	1988, Player	1966-74
22. **Cal Murphy**	2004, Builder	1997-99
23. **Don Narcisse**	2010, Player	1987-99
24. **Ken Preston**	1990, Builder	1940, 1943, 1946-48 (player) 1946-47 (HC), 1958-78 (GM)
25. **George Reed**	1979, Player	1963-75
26. **Dave Ridgway**	2003, Player	1982-95
27. **Al Ritchie**	1963, Builder	1921-24, 1930-32, 1935, 1942
28. **Rocco Romano**	2007, Player	1988
29. **Martin Ruby**	1974, Player	1951-57
30. **Willie Pless**	2005, Player	1999
31. **Tom Shepherd**	2008, Builder	1980-2005
32. **N.J. Taylor**	1963, Builder	1914-15, 1919, 1926-36
33. **Brian Timmis Sr.**	1963, Player	1920-22
34. **Ted Urness**	1989, Player	1961-70
35. **Clair Warner**	1965, Builder	1934-70

7 WW II Riders Honoured in the Pro Football Hall Fame

The U.S. Pro Football Hall of Fame opened its door on September 7, 1963, and is located in Canton, Ohio. The Hall's mission is to honour, preserve, educate and promote the rich traditions of American football.

At least seven American football players who served their country (the U.S.) in the Second World War went on to play for the Riders...

Name	Height, Position	Rider Years
1. **Frank Filchock**	5'11", Quarterback	1953 (as player
2. **Jim Keane**	6'4", End	1952
3. **Bob Nelson**	6'1", Centre	1951
4. **Martin Ruby**	6'4", Tackle	1951-57
5. **Jack Russell**	6'2", End	1951-52
6. **Mac Speedie**	6'3", Wide Receiver	1953-54
7. **John Wozniak**	6'0", Centre/LB	1953-56

We, the authors, acknowledge there are number of Rider players who fought for Canada during World War I and World War II. In fact, league play was often suspended throughout the nation during the war years because so many football players across Canada were serving their country.

We're working on a list of Riders who served in the Canadian armed forces. If you have any information on Riders that did so, when they played, and when they served our country, pass them along for a future edition! Contact: riderbookoflists@hotmail.com.

75 Other Halls of Fame with Rider Inductees

In addition to the Riders' Plaza of Honor, the Regina Sports Hall of Fame, and the Canadian Football Hall of Fame, here are 75 other Halls of Fame with Rider inductees...

Hall of Fame	Rider, Rider Position, Induction Year
1. **Acadia University Sports Hall of Fame**	Bob Vespaziani, Asst. GM – 1992
2. **Alabama Sports Hall of Fame**	Bobby Marlow, FB – 1986
3. **Alberta Sports Hall of Fame**	Cal Murphy, HC – 1997 Hugh Campbell, WR – 1997 Ron Estay, Coach – 1997
4. **Arizona State University Sports Hall of Fame**	Bobby Mulgado, RB – 1977 Freddie Williams, HB – 2002
5. **Augustana College Athletic Hall of Fame**	Heath Rylance, QB – 2007
6. **Baylor University Athletic Hall of Fame**	Larry Isbell, DB/P – 1975
7. **Bloomington Kennedy High School Athletic Hall of Fame**	Willis Jacox, WR/SB – 2007
8. **Bristol Sports Hall of Fame**	Al Benecick, OT – 2006
9. **BC Lions Wall of Fame**	Joe Paopao, QB – 2007
10. **Burlington-Edison High School Athletic Hall of Fame**	Garner Ekstran, DE – 2006
11. **Calgary Stampeders Wall of Fame**	Rocco Romano, G – 2008
12. **California Community College Football Coaches Association Hall of Fame**	Clyde "Lee" Grosscup, QB – 1988

Hall of Fame	Rider, Rider Position, Induction Year
13. **California State University (Long Beach) Athletics Hall of Fame**	Joe Paopao, QB – 2006
14. **Canadian Sports Hall of Fame**	Al Ritchie, Manager/HC – 1964 Brian Timmis Sr., RB – 1975 George Reed, RB – 1984 Ron Lancaster, QB/HC – 1985 Hugh Campbell, WR – 2009
15. **Cathedral High School Alumni Hall of Fame**	Rocco Romano, G – 2008
16. **CenCal Ballers Hall of Fame**	Chris DeFrance, WR – 2009 Dominique Dorsey, RB – 2008
17. **Clemson University Athletics Hall of Fame**	Homer Jordan, QB – 1993 Lester Brown, RB – 2007
18. **Colgate University Athletics Hall of Honour**	Tom Burgess, QB – 1986
19. **College Football Hall of Fame (USA)**	Glenn Dobbs, QB/P – 1980 Jeff Bentrim, QB – 1998
20. **Colorado Sports Hall of Fame**	Frank Tripucka, QB – 1983
21. **Concordia University Sports Hall of Fame**	Rocco Romano, G – 1988 Paul Vadja, G – 2001
22. **Denver Broncos Ring of Fame**	Frank Tripucka, QB/HC – 1986
23. **East Carolina University Athletics Hall of Fame**	Bill Cline, DB/QB – 1974
24. **Edmonton Eskimos Wall of Honour**	Hugh Campbell, WR – 1990 Willie Pless, LB – 1994
25. **Florence (North Carolina) Athletic Hall of Fame**	Joey Walters, WR – 2006 Darian Durant, QB – 2009
26. **Florida State University Hall of Fame**	Rhett Dawson, WR – 2006

Hall of Fame	Rider, Rider Position, Induction Year
27. **Hamilton Tiger Cats Wall of Fame**	Tom Clements, QB – 1994
28. **Holy Name High School Hall of Fame**	Bob Ptacek, QB/LB – 1976
29. **Los Gatos High School Athletic Hall of Fame**	Hugh Campbell, WR – 2004
30. **Manitoba Sports Hall of Fame**	Eddie James, HB – 2004 Gerry James, FB – 1982
31. **McNeese State University Athletics Hall of Fame**	Kerry Joseph, QB – 2006
32. **Mississauga Sports Council Hall of Fame**	Dwight Edwards, WR – 2000
33. **Montreal Alouettes Hall of Fame**	Cal Murphy, HC – 2004
34. **National Polish-American Sports Hall of Fame**	Frank Tripucka, QB/HC – 1997
35. **NCAA Division II Football Hall of Fame**	Jeff Bentrim, QB – 1999
36. **North Dakota State University Bison Athletic Hall of Fame**	Mike McTague, WR/P – 1990 Jeff Bentrim, QB – 2001
37. **Notre Dame-Cathedral Latin High School Alumni Hall of Fame**	John Paglio, T – 2006
38. **Oklahoma Sports Hall of Fame**	Glenn Dobbs, QB/P/HC – 1988 Steve Owen, HC – 2000
39. **Pacific University Athletic Hall of Fame**	Bob Light, WR – 1997
40. **Porterville College Athletic Hall of Fame**	Carm Carteri, LB – 2006
41. **Pro Football Hall of Fame**	Steve Owen, HC – 1966

Hall of Fame	Rider, Rider Position, Induction Year
42. **Redstone High School Black Hawk Football Hall of Fame**	Frank Filchock, QB/HC/GM
43. **Sam Houston State University Athletic Hall of Honour**	Matt Dominguez, WR – 2006
44. **Saskatchewan Sports Hall of Fame**	Al Ritchie, HC/Manager – 1966 George Reed, RB – 1979 Bill Clarke, DT – 1979 Ron Lancaster, QB/HC – 1981 John Alexander, Team Dr. – 1988 Dick Rendek, Executive – 1997 Roger Aldag, C/G – 2006 Tom Shepherd, Executive – 2009 Alan Ford, FB/WR/P/GM – 2010
45. **Saskatoon Sports Hall of Fame**	Kenneth "Dale" West, DB – 1986 Ron Atchison, DT – 1987 Dan Farthing, SB – 2004 Errol Brown, S – 2000 *(as part of 1990 Huskies team)* Jerry Friesen, LB/Coach – 2008
46. **Section V (New York State) Football Hall of Fame**	Tom Burgess, QB – 2000
47. **Sports Hall of Fame of New Jersey**	Frank Tripucka, QB/HC – 1999
48. **Texas A & M University Lettermen's Association Hall of Fame**	Martin Ruby, T – 1951-57 *– induction date unknown*
49. **Texas Sports Hall of Fame**	Larry Isbell, OE/DB/P – 2000
50. **Toronto Argonauts Hall of Fame**	Willie Pless, LB – 2000 Rocco Romano, G – 2007
51. **Tulane University Athletic Hall of Fame**	Carl "Nickie" Hall, QB – 1999 Frank Robinson, LB – 2001
52. **University of Florida Hall of Fame**	"Jimmy" Kynes, C – 1950 Doug Belden, QB – 1949

Hall of Fame	Rider, Rider Position, Induction Year
53. **University of Kansas Sports Hall of Fame**	Willie Pless, LB – 2000
54. **University of Kentucky Athletics Hall of Fame**	Craig Yeast, WR – 2006
55. **University of Miami Sports Hall of Fame**	Maurice Crum, LB – 2007
56. **University of Mississippi Athletics Hall of Fame**	Kent Austin, QB/HC – 2000
57. **University of North Dakota Letterwinners Association Hall of Fame**	Steve Myhra, LB/PK – 1976 Lawrie Skolrood, TE/OT – 2001
58. **University of Oregon Athletics Hall of Fame**	Vince Goldsmith, DE/LB – 2002
59. **University of Regina Sports Hall of Fame**	Jason Clermont, SB – 2007
60. **University of Saskatchewan Huskies Wall of Fame**	Jerry Friesen, LB/Coach – 1994 Dan Farthing, SB – 2001 (as part of team induction) Errol Brown, S – 2001 *(as part of team induction)*
61. **University of Tulsa Hall of Fame**	Glenn Dobbs, QB/P/HC – 1982
62. **University of Utah Crimson Club Hall of Fame**	Mac Curtis Speedie, WR – 1986 Clyde "Lee" Grosscup, QB – 1990
63. **Utah Sports Hall of Fame**	Mac Curtis Speedie, WR – 1972 Jack Hill, RB/WR – 1982
64. **Washington Sports Hall of Fame**	George Reed, RB – 1983 Hugh Campbell, WR – 1994 Vince Goldsmith, DE – 2005
65. **Washington State University Athletic Hall of Fame**	Hugh Campbell, WR – 1978 George Reed, RB – 1978

Hall of Fame	Rider, Rider Position, Induction Year
66. **Watertown High School Athletic Hall of Fame**	Heath Rylance, QB – 2002
67. **Weber State University Athletics Hall of Fame**	Ron McCall, TE – 1992
68. **Webster Groves High School Statesman Sports Hall of Fame**	Tracey Mack, LB – 1980
69. **West Seneca Central Schools Athletics Wall of Fame**	Kevin Mason, QB – 1998
70. **West Texas A&M University Hall of Champions**	Alondra Johnson, LB – 2005
71. **Western Michigan University Athletic Hall of Fame**	Pete Wysocki, LB – 1993
72. **Western Kentucky University Athletics Hall of Fame**	Eagle "Buddy" Keys, HC – 1994
73. **Whitworth University Heritage Gallery Hall of Fame**	Hugh Campbell, WR – 1998
74. **Winnipeg Football Club Hall of Fame**	Eddie James, HB – 1984 Gerry James, FB – 1984 Cal Murphy, HC – 2002 Greg Battle, LB – 2001 Tom Clements, QB – 1992
75. **Wittenberg University Athletic Hall of Honour**	Ron Lancaster, QB – 1985 Jim Worden, TE – 1988

We, the authors, gratefully acknowledge the inductee information and data provided by the above Halls of Fame through their websites ...and encourage readers to take a "virtual visit" of these halls to see what you can find!

If you know of any other Halls of Fame, no matter how big or small, prominent or obscure, which have inducted Riders – pass them along for future a edition! Contact: riderbookoflists@hotmail.com

IV. We Walk Among You: The Riders & Pop Culture

Featuring...

Six Degrees of Rider Nation

Six Degrees of Rider Nation
The Riders & Ashton Kutcher

This fun series of lists was developed to play off of the concept of 'Six Degrees of Separation.' The concept theorizes every person is no more than six steps away from any other person, such that a chain of "a friend of a friend" type of statements can connect any two people in the world.

So, here is the connection – in six or fewer steps – between...

The Riders and Actor Ashton Kutcher:

1. **Ashton Kutcher**, television and film actor and producer, starred in the romantic comedy *Coming Soon* (1999). You may also remember him as "Michael Kelso" in the television sitcom *That 70's Show*.

2. In addition to Kutcher, actor **Ryan O'Neal** was among the cast in the movie *Coming Soon*.

3. Actor Ryan O'Neal was romantically involved with actress **Farrah Fawcett**.

4. Farrah Fawcett starred in the hit television series (from 1976-81) ***Charlie's Angels***.

5. 1977 Rider running back **Tommy Reamon** acted in several episodes of the television series *Charlie's Angels* between 1979 and 1981, *North Dallas Forty* (1979), and *Quincy M.E.* (1979). Reamon played six games with the Riders in 1977; rushing 78 times for 411 yards (5.3 yard avg.), longest 61 yards, and three touchdowns.

   Prior to his stint with the Riders, Reamon was drafted by the Pittsburgh Steelers in the 9th round (223rd overall) of the 1974 NFL Draft. He played with the Florida Blazers (1974) and the Jacksonville Express (1975) of the World Football League that folded after two seasons (1974-75). He went on to play for the NFL's Kansas City Chiefs in 1976. Reamon also co-wrote a book titled *The Rough Diamonds: A Coach's Journey*, published in 2003.

Six Degrees of Rider Nation
The Riders & Jerry Seinfeld

Just as before, playing off of the concept of 'Six Degrees of Separation' theorizing everyone is no more than six steps away from any other, here is the connection – in six or fewer steps – between...

The Riders and Actor, Comedian Jerry Seinfeld:

1. American actor and stand-up comedian **Jerry Seinfeld** played a fictional version of himself the hit U.S. television network NBC show *Seinfeld* (1989-98).

2. A fellow cast member of Seinfeld's was **Jerry Stiller**, who played the neurotic and abrasive character "Frank Constanza."

3. Jerry Stiller's son is actor **Ben Stiller**. Ben Stiller appeared in movies such as *Tropic Thunder* (2008), *Meet the Fockers* (2004), and ***There's Something About Mary*** (1998) to name just a few.

4. Among the cast of *There's Something About Mary*, Ben Stiller was joined by sport celebrity **Brett Favre**, who played himself. Favre of course is none other than the famed NFL quarterback who played most of his career with the **Green Bay Packers**, though played the 2009 season with the Minnesota Vikings.

5. For several years while Favre was at the helm of the Green Bay Packers, his quarterbacks coach from 2006-07 was none other than former Rider quarterback **Tom Clements** (1979). At the time of writing, Tom Clements was still coaching with the Packers.

21 Rider Inspired Books/Publications

Since the truth is often stranger than fiction, it's no surprise the Riders lead in published material...Here are twenty-one publications inspired in whole or in part by the Riders...

1. ***92 Years of Roughrider Football***, by Edward Yuen (2002); published by the author.
2. ***The Greatest Grey Cup Ever! 1989: Before, Then & After,*** by Rob Vanstone (2010); Regina Leader-Post Carrier Foundation.
3. ***Green Grit – An Illustrated History of the Saskatchewan Roughriders,*** by Graham Kelly (2001); HarperCollins Canada.
4. ***Green Magic - Canada's Team Wins the 2007 Grey Cup!,*** by the *Voice of the Riders* Rod Pedersen (2008); published by Lulu Publishing and the Saskatchewan Roughriders.
5. ***The Grey Cup: A History***, by Graham Kelly (1999); Johnson Gorman Publishers. *Kelly was a waterboy and assistant equipment manager with the Riders before becoming a newspaper columnist. His book focuses on key Grey Cup matchups and contains a chapter entitled "Saskatchewan and Ottawa: On Roughriders!"*
6. ***Gridiron Greats of Saskatchewan,*** by Louise Froggett (1995); published by the Canadian Football Hall of Fame.
7. ***Heroes of the Game: A History of the Grey Cup***, by Stephen Thiele (1997); Moulin Publishing. *This book provides a historical context and summary of every Grey Cup game up to 1997. It contains a chapter: "Regina Fails to Win the Cup" that focuses on the Roughriders' six Grey Cup appearances from 1928 to 1934.*
8. ***Legends of Autumn: The Glory Years of Canadian Football***, by Denny Boyd and Brian Scrivener (1997); Greystone Books. *This book features a chapter on every CFL team in the 1950s and 1960s and. The Riders' chapter is entitled "Local Heroes."*
9. ***Rider Pride: The Story of Canada's Best-Loved Football Team,*** by Bob Calder and Garry Andrews (1984); Western Producer Prairie Books.

10. ***Rider Pride on the American Side: A Minnesota Family Discovers the Saskatchewan Roughriders,*** by Terry McEvoy, foreword by Dave Ridgway and Roy Shivers (2006); Lulu publishing.

11. ***Rider Pride on the American Side: A Minnesota Family Discovers the Saskatchewan Roughriders – Grey Cup Edition,*** by Terry McEvoy, with special contributions by Dustin Cherniawski and Dave Ridgway (2008); Northern Road Press.

12. ***Robokicker: An odyssey through the CFL,*** by Dave Ridgway with David Poulsen (1995); Johnson Gorman Publishers (1995).

13. ***Saskatchewan Roughriders 1910-1980 Club Record and Information Book,*** by the Saskatchewan Roughriders (1980); published by the Saskatchewan Roughrider Football Club.

14. ***Saskatchewan Roughriders First 100 Years,*** by Bob Calder, Gordon Staseson, Julie Folk, Bob Hughes, Rob Vanstone. Darrell Davis, Dan Marce (2009); Regina Leader-Post Carrier Foundation.

15. ***Saskatchewan Roughrider Player Reference 1960-1996,*** by Curt Phillips (1997); published by the author.

16. ***Third and Long: Inside the CFL***, by Willie Thomas (1987); Western Producer Prairie Books. *Thomas' account of his ten year CFL career. He spent 1985 with the Riders (Guard), and a chapter of the book is on the training camp he attended in Saskatoon.*

17. ***Touchdown cooking: Championship Recipes,*** by the Saskatchewan Roughrider Touchdown Cooking Committee (1995); published by Saskatchewan Roughrider Touchdown Cooking.

18. ***Touchdown Cooking, Grey Cup Edition: Championship Recipes,*** by the Saskatchewan Roughrider Touchdown Cooking Committee (1999), Centax Books & Distribution.

19. ***Touchdown Cooking: Winning Recipes from Saskatchewan Roughriders Past and Present***, by the Saskatchewan Roughrider Touchdown Cooking Committee (1985); published by Saskatchewan Roughrider Touchdown Cooking.

20. ***West Riders Best - 1966: Before, Then & After*** by Rob Vanstone (2009); Regina Leader-Post Carrier Foundation.

21. ***The Rider Book of Lists: 100 Lists Honouring 100 Years of the Saskatchewan Roughriders***, by Rod Nasewich and Sheldon Green (2010); published by the authors.

Green on the Screen!
Riders on the Big & Little Screens

No, this isn't about the Maxtron at Mosaic Stadium. Here are some TV shows and films in which a Rider appeared or the Riders were featured...

1. **The Simpsons: Season 3, Episode 7F23 "When Flanders Failed" (1991)**
   This episode originally aired on October 3, 1991, and revolved around Ned Flanders quitting his job and opening the doomed "Leftorium" - a store selling items for left handed people. Instead of attending Flanders' invitation BBQ where he announces the opening of the Leftorium, Homer is on his couch watching the CFL Draft - the 15th round no less, and the announcer in the background can be heard referring to the Saskatchewan Roughriders who *"scored only four rouges all season."* Calgary, Edmonton and BC are also mentioned.
2. **South Park: Season 2, Episode 1, "April Fool's" (1998)**
   This episode aired on Comedy Central on April 1, 1998, and featured Terrance and Phillip foiling a plot by Saddam Hussein to take over Canada at a 'RoughRiders vs RoughRiders' game at Canada Stadium. The game's announcer is heard to say: *"...and the RoughRiders are really giving the RoughRiders a run for their money; all else aside the RoughRiders are really out-matched by these RoughRiders."*
3. **Columbo: "A Bird in the Hand" (1992)**
   This 2-hour TV movie aired November 22, 1992, and featured Peter Falk as Columbo investigating the death (murder) of a football team owner. The football team was "The Stallions" and footage from a Saskatchewan Roughrider-Edmonton Eskimo game was used with Saskatchewan's 'S' standing for the Stallions. When the movie required play action, it used footage of Kent Austin in his #5 jersey, and the actor quarterback used the number throughout the movie. It also starred actors Steve Forrest, Greg Evigan, and Tyne Daly.
4. **CFL Traditions: Saskatchewan Roughrider Edition "Tales of Grey Cups & Glory" (2003)**
   CFL Traditions was a 10 episode series, produced by Network Entertainment, and aired on TSN in 2003. Episode one covers the origins of Canadian football, and the remaining detail the history of each CFL team through interviews with players and archival footage.

5. **Football First: The Roy Shivers Story (2004)**
This documentary on former Rider General Manager Roy Shivers was produced by CBC Saskatchewan and aired on CBC in November, 2004, both locally and nationally. It covers Shivers' early years in a segregated Arkansas and his growing up in West Oakland alongside others who would become famous black athletes and activists. It profiles his career as a football player in the 1950s, his interracial marriage, and his becoming the first black general manager in professional football. It was nominated for two Gemini Awards

6. **"What it's Like to Bleed Green" - Valerie Pringle has Left the Building (2005)**
This CTV Travel and Outdoor Life Network series features Valerie Pringle profiling exotic destinations, great journeys and colourful cultures throughout the world. In season three, she focuses on her own backyard - Canada - including Saskatchewan. In this episode, Pringle stacks hay, floats in the "Dead Sea" of Saskatchewan (Lake Manitou), meets up with Brent Butt, and experiences Rider Pride with Corey Holmes, Marcus Crandell and the Labour Day Classic.

7. **The Little General: The Life and Times of Ron Lancaster (2006)**
"Life & Times" was a CBC series featuring biographies of prominent Canadians that ran from 1996 to 2006. Its final season featured a biography of Rider great Ron Lancaster and aired on Saturday, June 24, 2006. The bio covers Lancaster's Pennsylvania roots, his high school and university football days, and his almost half century in the CFL as a quarterback, head coach, broadcaster, and general manager.

8. **The Rick Mercer Report: Rough Ride (2006)**
This episode aired on CBC on October 3, 2006 and features Mercer practicing with the Riders (in full gear thanks to Norm Fong) and kibbutzing with Gene Makowsky, Scott Schultz, Rob Lazeo, Jeremy O'Day, and Luca Congi. He attends a tailgate party and his first ever CFL game (against BC played on September 24, 2006 – the Riders won 23-20). There is also a spoof 'Made for TV Movie' about the life and times of Piffles Taylor, starring Mercer as Taylor.

9. **Legends of the Palouse (2006)**
This series of films profiles the Washington State University (WSU) Football team, the Cougars, along with its greatest players and the alumni attachment to the school. The movies feature commentary by various sports celebrities including Hugh Campbell who played for the Cougars from 1960-62 and led the nation in receiving, and George Reed, WSU running back from 1959, 1961-62.

10. **Season of Dreams (2007)**
This feature-length documentary by Five Stones Films of Saskatoon is about Saskatchewan's love affair with football. It uses as a backdrop the 2006 seasons of the Riders, a rural six-man team from Hague, and an urban twelve-man team from Saskatoon. The film also features interviews with Rider legends such as George Reed, Ron Lancaster, Ron Atchison, and Roger Aldag, as well as sports broadcasters Glen Suitor, Chris Cuthbert, Brian Williams, Chris Walby, and Steve Armitage. The film aired on TSN in October 2008 and is available for purchase on DVD.

11. **Corner Gas: Season 6, Episode 8, "Reader Pride" (2009)**
Almost every episode of Corner Gas has someone in Rider logowear, usually the character Hank Yarbo, but this episode from the series' final season is all about 'gearing' up Rider style, as Brent competes with Lacey and Hank to show he's a true Rider fan. The episode features cameos by Matt Dominguez and Gene Makowsky and a couple of memorable lines like "I've been a fan of the Riders since they moved from Ottawa", and "Molly McGee was quite a woman...the first female to play in the CFL." Another notable episode is Season 1, Episode 13: 'I Love Lacey', where the whole gang is on their way, two by two, to the Grey Cup in Regina, but no one quite makes it to the big game.

12. **In the Huddle (Present)**
In the Huddle, produced by Access Communications of Regina, airs every Tuesday during football season. Current and former "Voice of the Riders" sportscasters Rod Peterson and John Lynch are joined by a roster of guests to discuss the Riders' fortunes each week. Each show features a viewer call in, player and coach interviews, the rules of the game, and next week's predictions.

13. **Riders to the Max (Present)**
Riders to the Max is a bi-weekly show during the football season on Channel 48, SaskTel Max Local On Demand, with Rider player and coach interviews and other features on the team.

14. **North Dallas Forty (1979), Charlie's Angels, Quincy M.E.**
Tommy Reamon was a Rider running back in 1977 after bouncing around the NFL and WFL. He played six games with the Riders in 1977; rushing 78 times for 411 yards (5.3 yard avg.), longest 61 yards, and three touchdowns. After his time with the Riders, he acted in several episodes of the television series Charlie's Angels between 1979 and 1981, North Dallas Forty (1979), and Quincy M.E. (1979).

15. **The Best Little Whorehouse in Texas (1982)**
Included in the cast of this movie, among the likes of Dolly Parton, Burt Reynolds and Dom DeLuise, was Clyde "Lee" Grosscup playing the role of "Football Color Man." Grosscup was also a part of a large cast of Rider quarterbacks in the 1963 season; unfortunately for him it was the beginning of the Ron Lancaster era. The Riders' 1963 season saw five quarterbacks in action, led by Lancaster, with Frank Tripucka, Bob Ptacek, M.C. Reynolds, and Grosscup. Before joining the Riders in 1963, Grosscup played the previous three seasons for the NFL's New York Jets. Grosscup went on to become a long serving sports broadcaster in the USA, when in 1966 he began a forty year television and radio broadcasting career on NBC, ABC and local radio covering the NFL, college football, and the USFL.

16. **The Garbage Picking Field Goal Kicking Philadelphia Phenomenon (1998)**
Mike Vanderjagt appeared in this Walt Disney television movie as the kicking stand-in for Actor Tony Danza. Vanderjagt played in a couple of games for the Riders in 1993, as a punter, alongside placekicker Dave Ridgway. After the Riders, Vanderjagt played in the Arena Football League in 1996, had another stint in the CFL in Toronto, then went on to the NFL for two different teams. He ended up in 2008 back in Toronto for one season.

17. **Shipbuilder (1985)**
This short film, produced by the National Film Board of Canada and written by Saskatchewan writer and playwright Ken Mitchell, depicts the true story of Tom Sukanen, a Finnish immigrant who homesteaded in the 1920s and 1930s in the Macrorie-Birsay area of Saskatchewan. Sukanen spent about a decade of his life constructing and moving overland a small ship that was to carry him back to Finland. He never did sail his ship, and he died in the 1940s. In the film, Tom Sukanen is played by former Rider Galen Wahlmeier (Centre/Long snapper/Linebacker, 1957, 1959-63, 1965-67).

18. **The Saskatchewan Roughriders Documentary – The First 100 Years (2010)**
This documentary commemorating the Riders' 100th anniversary is in production by Regina-based (and Emmy award winning) multi-media production and distribution company Partners In Motion. The documentary will feature interviews and re-enactments of famous Rider moments from the team's 100 years of lore and legend. It is anticipated to be broadcast in Fall 2010 and available on DVD.

Six Degrees of Rider Nation
The Riders & Alec Baldwin

Just as before, here is the connection – in six or fewer steps – between…

The Riders and Actor Alec Baldwin:

1. American actor **Alec Baldwin** has worked in movies, theatre and television. Among his many credits are TV shows *Knots Landing, Friends, Will and Grace*, the current sitcom *30 Rock*, and movies *It's Complicated* (2009), *The Aviator* (2004), *The Cooler* (2003), *Pearl Harbour* (2001), and *The Hunt for Red October* (1999).

2. USA based NBC television's ***Saturday Night Live*** is a late-night sketch comedy and variety show taped live each week. The show, created in 1975 by Canadian born Lorne Michaels (the show's current executive producer), has featured Actor Alec Baldwin as its guest host more than a dozen times. Over his 35 years at the helm of the show, Lorne Michaels has brought on board guest hosts from all sorts of backgrounds, and in 2007 popular NFL quarterback **Payton Manning** (Indianapolis Colts since 1998) opened the show with the trade mark line "*Live from New York, it's Saturday Night*!"

3. In 2001 Payton Manning's quarterbacks coach with the Indianapolis Colts was none other than former Rider quarterback (1980-83, 1987) **John Hufnagel**.

   Just for fun, this list could have taken a few more degrees with . . .

4. Payton Manning's younger brother is **Eli Manning**, a great quarterback in his own right with the NFL's New York Giants.

5. While Eli Manning has been with the New York Giants, the team's offensive coordinator from 2004-06 was also **John Hufnagel** or Another connection is current Giants offensive coordinator **Kevin Gilbride**, who replaced Hufnagel, was an assistant coach with the defunct Ottawa Rough Riders from 1984-86. While in Ottawa, Gilbride would have gotten to know a quarterback who played for Ottawa that year by the name of **Tom Burgess**. Burgess was a Rider quarterback from 1987-89 and 1994-95.

Six Degrees of Rider Nation
The Riders & Elvis

Here is the connection – in six or fewer steps – between...

The Riders and The King – Elvis Presley:

1. A man that needs no introduction, **Elvis Presley** is The King of Rock 'n' Roll. Presley is a cultural icon and considered one of the most popular American singers of the 20th century. "Elvis" died at the age of 42 in 1977.

2. In the wake of the assassination in 1968 of U.S. President Robert "Bobby" Kennedy, then President **Lyndon B. Johnson** ordered Secret Service protection for all presidential and vice presidential candidates.

3. Being the iconic personality he was, Elvis was able to open doors to the corridors of power. In a somewhat bizarre event in 1971, Elvis orchestrated a meeting at the White House with U.S. President **Richard Nixon**. Nixon was the 37th President of the USA, from 1969- 1974.

4. U.S. President Richard Nixon's Vice President was **Spiro Agnew** (1969-73). Prior to winning the Vice Presidency, Agnew was the Governor of Maryland.

5. Vice President Spiro Agnew would be provided with a security detail of Secret Service personnel. One of the individuals to land a job in the expanding ranks of the U.S. Secret Service was Rider **Roger Ellis** (guard, 1964). Ellis saw action in three games in 1964, with the likes of Lancaster throwing most of the passes, Ed Buchanan running the ball more often than George Reed, and Hugh Campbell leading the receiving corps with an even 1,000 yards.

Riders on the Charts
10 Pop Songs & Albums Inspired by the Riders

1. **"Paint The Whole World Green"** – lyrics and music by Jason Plumb (2007)
   In 2007, the Roughriders commissioned Regina-based singer/songwriter Jason Plumb to write a theme song for the team on route to its third Grey Cup title. Plumb's "Paint The Whole World Green" became a popular anthem in the community, and across Canada on the worldwide web. It can be found on the 2009 CD *Wide Open Music: Songs for Saskatchewan* by Jason Plumb and The Willing.

2. **"True North Strong & Green" (The Saskatchewan Roughrider Song)** – lyrics and music by Dean Kush/Faster Gun (2005)
   Written and performed by Regina-based country music band, Faster Gun, this song is dedicated to all those hardcore and hard working Roughrider fans. The band has performed it at Labour Day games, Riderville and other Grey Cup festivities, at the Craven Country Music Jamboree, and the Saskatchewan Country Music Awards. The song can be found on the band's 2007 CD *Back Again* that won the Saskatchewan Country Music Award (SCMA) for Album of the Year in 2007.

3. **"Huddle Up in Saskatchewan"** – Jay Robertson (1995)
   This song was commissioned for the 1995 Grey Cup, the first held in Regina. Committee organizers used the 'Huddle Up' theme for several reasons – first, it was going to be cold (and boy was it!) and second, hotel rooms would be scarce so billeting and staying with friends and family would be essential to accommodate the 52,564 who would attend the game. Saskatchewan-based artists Jay Robertson, Darcy Dolejsi, Stan Garchinski, Jack Semple, Brad Johner, and the Saskatchewan Express performed on the song, which, although written for the Grey Cup, makes references to the Roughriders and Rider Pride.

4. **"Flat Out in Saskatchewan"** – lyrics and music by Wide Mouth Mason (2003)
   This song and its title was the theme for the second Grey Cup to be held in Regina in 2003. It was written and performed by Saskatoon's Wide Mouth Mason and makes reference to the world's best fans going flat out in the flatlands. It's unknown if the song was ever released on an album.

5. **"Twist & Shout, Saskatchewan!"** – produced by Brendan Cross & Mark Schmidt (1997)
   This tribute song based on the Beatles' classic was performed and recorded by Brendan Cross & The Bart's on Broad All-Star Band in the summer of 1997, the year the Riders made it to the Grey Cup against Toronto. The song can be found on the internet.

6. ***Green is the Colour* (Album)** – recorded by members of the Saskatchewan Roughriders (1983).
   This album, recorded in the early 1980s by a cast of Rider players (and their wives) singing such songs as Cover of the Leader-Post, Roughrider Sound, Drop Kick Me Jesus, Six Days on the Road, The Gopher-It Song, and of course, Green is the Colour. The list of those on vocals includes Bob Poley, Roger Aldag, Lawrie Skolrood, Ken Clark, Carm Carteri, Mike Samples (doing a solo on The Milk Song), Steve Mazurak, Lyall Woznesensky, Marshall Hamilton, and a number of others. It was produced by Gridiron Pride and recorded at DK Musical Services. While the actual album might be tough to find, versions of some of the songs can be found on the internet.

7. ***800 lbs of West Country Rock* (Album)** – recorded by Brock, Bailey and Roth (1970)
   This is an album of well known country music songs recorded by three larger members of the Roughriders: Clyde Brock (offensive tackle), Nolan Bailey (tight end) and Tim Roth (defensive tackle) who played for the team in the 1970s. Produced by Buffalo Records, the album cover features the three in full Rider gear and the record features the songs: "Me & Bobby McGee", "Six Days on the Road", "Ribbon of Darkness" and "Kawliga." Copies can be found for purchase on the internet

8. **"The Roughrider Anthem"** – recorded by Frontlyne (2003)
   Frontlyne formed in 2003 and included Riders Shonte Peoples (defensive end), Nealon Green (quarterback), and Kenton Keith (running back). The band played rap and hip hop at university pubs in the province and recorded an album featuring raps about the Riders, football and players getting ready for game day.

9. **Remixes: "Spirit in the Sky (Rider Pride)", "We Love Rider Football", "Bust the Cats", "Endzone Satisfaction"**
These are just some of the spoof remakes of popular songs with Rider-inspired lyrics. The first one is sung to the tune of Norman Greenbaum's original Spirit in the Sky, the second to Queen's We Will Rock You, the third to Young MC's Bust a Move, and the fourth to the Stones' song Satisfaction. Various versions of these can be found bootlegged on CD and internet sites.

10. ***Canadian Football Songs* (Album)** – recorded by Dal Richards (1968)
This album was recorded by longtime and legendary Vancouver bandleader Dal Richards who began his career in the 1930s and still plays concerts (including at the 2010 Winter Olympics). He produced half-time shows for the BC Lions, and in this capacity he made the Canadian Football Songs album that was sold in stores and distributed to Canadian radio stations for airplay during football games. The album features all CFL team fight songs including "On Roughriders!", the lyrics for which Richards adapted from "On Wisconsin" (see the list *Rider Cheer Songs & Their Lyrics*).

Rider Retailing – From A to Z

Here are some of the more unusual items emblazoned with the Rider logo available at The Rider Store online or at three locations in Regina and Saskatoon, as well as other online and in-store retailers across the province and across the country...

A - 'apps' (free for compatible mobile devices, contact your provider)
B - beerbox (Pilsner) cowboy hat ($18.18), bag chairs (29.99) and bikinis ($39.99)
C - cribbage games ($39.95), cutting boards ($59.99 - wood)
D - desk lamps ($29.95)
E - elevator pens ($7.99)
F - foam watermelonheads ($54.95) or melon hats ($33.95)
G - garden gnomes ($49.95-$59.95)
H - hot sauce ($7.49) or hacky sacks ($3.95)
I - inflatable chairs ($59.95) and inflatable players ($138.99)
J - jersey napkins ($5.95/set of 8) or jersey bathroom mats ($59.99)
K - key chains ($8.95)
L - lip balm ($4.50) (there is also dental floss for $5.99)
M - mouse pads ($13.99) and mouse ($29.95)
N - nite lights ($5.99) or light switch plates ($5.99)
O - onesie, bib and bootie sets ($24.95)
P - puppets (Gainer $24.95), pillows ($29.95) and potato chips ($1.79)
Q - BBQ covers ($109.95, jersey style - $69.95)
R - ringtones ($3.50 - contact your SaskTel cellular service provider)
S - scoreboard clock and calendar ($149.99) or desk size ($79.99)
T - thermoses - soup, coffee or other beverages ($10.00-$12.00)
U - umbrellas ($34.95)
V - Victorinox Swiss Army watches ($399.00)
W - whiskey ($29.99) or wine ($12.99) or windshield washer fluid (green of course – $4.99)
X - x-mas ornaments ($9.95)
Y - yo-yos ($3.99)
Z - zip drives ($19.99)

Prices as of May 1, 2010.

Six Degrees of Rider Nation
The Riders & The Donald

Just as before, playing off of the concept of 'Six Degrees of Separation' that theorizes everyone is no more than six steps away from any other, here is the connection – in six or fewer steps – between...

The Riders and The Donald (Donald Trump):

1. **Donald Trump**, real estate and business magnate, and entertainment personality, is the Executive Producer and Host of the popular reality television show ***The Celebrity Apprentice***.

2. Appearing in the 2010 season of *The Celebrity Apprentice* (and 'fired' in week six) was **Bill Goldberg** who has been active in the acting business since the late 1990's. Goldberg is probably best known as a professional sports entertainment wrestling star, though he was drafted into the NFL in 1990 and saw some playing time as a Defensive End with the Atlanta Falcons from 1992-94. He also spent time on the off-season or practice roster of the LA Rams and Carolina Panthers.

3. Bill Goldberg married **Wanda Ferraton** in 2005. Wanda Goldberg (nee Ferraton), entrepreneur, stunt double, and television show host, was **Miss Saskatchewan Roughrider 1992**. She was raised in Montmarte, Saskatchewan.

Six Degrees of Rider Nation
The Riders & JFK

Here we go again...

The Riders and JFK (U.S. President John F. Kennedy):

1. U.S. President **John F. Kennedy** in 1962 appointed **Byron White** as a U.S. Supreme Court judge. Prior to the appointment, White practiced law for many years and also worked in the U.S. Department of Justice.

2. **Byron "Whizzer" White** was also a standout running back with NFL football's Detroit Lions (1940-41), leading the NFL in rushing in both seasons. White was also inducted into the U.S. College Football Hall of Fame.

3. The 1941 Detroit Lions' head coach was **Bill Edwards**. Edwards also coached at the college ranks, and for his coaching contribution was inducted into the U.S. College Football Hall of Fame in 1986 (along with notable NFL coach Mike Ditka).

4. While coaching (1955-68) at **Wittenburg University** (Springfield, Ohio, USA), Bill Edwards coached none other than Rider legend, The Little General, **Ron Lancaster** (Wittenburg Class of 1960).

Log In & Often
The Riders & Social Networking

The Riders and the Rider Nation have embraced social networking in a big way. Twitter followers (T) may be lagging some other CFL teams a bit, but the Riders lead the league with Facebook (FB) friends...

Team/League	Followers
1. **Saskatchewan Roughriders:**	34,175 (FB); 2,078 (T)
2. **Montreal Alouettes:**	20,862 (FB); 3,642 (T)
3. **British Columbia Lions:**	12,341 (FB); 3,059 (T)
4. **CFL**	10,394 (FB); 5,675 (T)
5. **Hamilton Tiger-Cats:**	7,957 (FB); 1,282 (T)
6. **Winnipeg Blue Bombers:**	5,645 (FB); 1,041 (T)
7. **Calgary Stampeders:**	4,277 (FB); 2,280 (T)
8. **Edmonton Eskimos:**	3,363 (FB); 2,125 (T)
9. **Toronto Argonauts:**	448 (FB); 2,701 (T)

As of July 4, 2010 (except Edmonton FB followers - April 7, 2010).

Six Degrees of Rider Nation
The Riders & The Queen

Here is the connection – in six or fewer steps – between...

The Riders and Her Majesty Queen Elizabeth II:

1. **Queen Elizabeth II**, Queen of Canada, in 1973 appointed The Right Honourable **Jules Léger** Canada's 21st Governor General. Léger held that appointment from 1974-1979.

2. The Governor General awards select Canadian citizens the **Order of Canada** (at various levels). The GG's website indicates the Order "is the centrepiece of Canada's honours system and recognizes a lifetime of outstanding achievement, dedication to the community and service to the nation. The Order recognizes people in all sectors of Canadian society."

3. Léger in 1978 invested a new **Member of the Order of Canada** on a person who also just happened to be the best running back in CFL history; and in case you haven't guessed it yet, it was none other than a Rider of unparalleled acclaim, number 34, **George Robert Reed**, BSc., CM.

   Note: Another individual involved in the Roughriders' organization who was made a Member of the Order of Canada was **Gordon Staseson**, in 2005. Among Staseson's many accomplishments and contributions include serving as president of the Riders from 1979 to 1982, and chairman of the CFL Board of Governors in 1983.

Six Degrees of Rider Nation
The Riders & Dolly Parton

Here is the connection – in six or fewer steps – between...

The Riders and Dolly Parton:

1. **Dolly Parton**, country music superstar, actress, and entrepreneur, starred in several movies. Parton is best known for her country music contribution. One movie Parton played a leading role in was ***The Best Little Whorehouse in Texas***, in 1982. The movie was a filmization of the Broadway musical of the same name in which a sheriff (and regular whorehouse patron), fights to keep a historical whorehouse open.

2. The cast of *The Best Little Whorehouse in* Texas included the likes of Burt Reynolds and Dom DeLuise. Among the cast was **Clyde "Lee" Grosscup** playing the role of "Football Color Man." Earlier in his life, Grosscup joined a large cast of quarterbacks in the Riders' 1963 season; although unfortunately for him it was the beginning of the Ron Lancaster era. In addition to Grosscup, the Riders' 1963 season saw five quarterbacks in action, led by Lancaster with support from Frank Tripucka, Bob Ptacek, M.C. Reynolds, and Grosscup. Grosscup had played the previous three seasons (1960, 61 and 62) for the NFL's New York Jets before being released and moving up north to join the Riders in 1963. Grosscup went on to become a long-serving sports broadcaster in the USA, beginning in 1966 a forty year television and radio broadcasting career on NBC, ABC and local radio covering the NFL, college football, and the USFL (see the list *13 Riders Who Became Sportscasters).*

Six Degrees of Rider Nation
The Riders & General MacArthur

Here is the connection – in six or fewer steps – between...

The Riders and U.S. General Douglas MacArthur:

1. Prominent historical American military figure **General Douglas MacArthur** was the Chief of Staff of the U.S. Army in the 1930s and played a key role in the South Pacific theatre during the WW II.

2. In 1937 a Texan by the name of **Lyndon B. Johnson** was elected to the U.S. House of Representatives from the Texas 10th District; a position he held until 1949. After the U.S. joined WW II, Johnson, still in Congress, became an officer in the Naval Reserve. In 1942, President Franklin Delano Roosevelt appointed Johnson to a survey team to monitor military activities in the South Pacific. On this assignment Johnson reported to General MacArthur in Australia.

3. Following the War, Johnson became a U.S. Senator (1949-61). In 1961, he became the U.S. Vice President (1961-63) under President **John F. Kennedy**. With the assassination of Kennedy in November 1963, LBJ became the 36th President of the United States.

4. **C. Farris Bryant** was appointed in 1969 by President Johnson to serve on the United States National Security Council and in the White House Office of Emergency Planning. Prior to this, Bryant spent a four year term as the Governor of Florida from 1964-69.

5. During Bryant's term as Florida Governor, **James W. "Jimmy" Kynes** was elected to the position of Florida Attorney General. Kynes would later be appointed to the Florida Supreme Court.

6. In 1950, the Riders had a 7-7 season under Head Coach Fred Grant. Along with Rider greats Ken Charlton, Len Ortman, Bob Pelling, Sully Glasser, Del Wardien, Toar Springstein, and Jack Hartman, was a football and baseball standout from the University of Florida - **Jimmy Kynes**. Kynes would play just one season of professional football, as centre with the Riders, before returning to Florida to earn a law degree and become a prominent public figure.

Six Degrees of Rider Nation
The Riders & Oprah

Here we go again with...

The Riders and Oprah:

1. American television talk show host, actress, and media giant **Oprah Gail Winfrey** created the popular day-time television show *The Oprah Winfrey Show* in 1986. A few of her creative endeavours include her own media production company Harpo Films, *O, The Oprah Magazine*, Oprah Radio and the Oprah Book Club.

2. ***The Oprah Winfrey Show*** has introduced audiences to an incredible array of topics, celebrities, and other historic and pop culture personalities. After appearances on *Oprah*, **Philip Calvin McGraw** became an American TV personality. Best known as **Dr. Phil**, McGraw is a psychologist, talk show host, and author. The *Dr. Phil Show* debuted on American television in 2002.

3. In 1968, Phil McGraw was awarded a football scholarship to the **University of Tulsa**. McGraw played middle linebacker in 1968, but would finish his college at another institution. From 1961-68, the Tulsa Golden Hurricane team was coached by Rider great **Glenn Dobbs**. Dobbs was a Rider quarterback and punter for three seasons, 1951-53, as well as the head coach in 1952.

   On November 23, 1968, the Tulsa Golden Hurricane football team, including McGraw, Dobbs as coach and Dobbs' son Johnny, was handed one of the worst defeats in U.S. college history, losing 100-6 against the Houston Cougars in front of 34,008 spectators in the Houston Astrodome. It was said the Tulsa team was impacted by the flu and injuries; Dobbs reportedly fell ill in the days before the game, missing two days of practice. The Tulsa locker room was said to look more like a MASH unit at half time, and as the starting quarterback was no longer fit to play, Dobbs' son Johnny played quarterback in the second half. It is said Tulsa fans still harbour resentment toward Houston Cougars' coach Bill Yeoman for running up the score so badly. One of the Houston athletes who caught a touchdown pass, the only major of his college career, was future country music performer Larry Gatlin.

V. Overtime: More Curious Information for the Rider Nation

100 Saskatchewan-born Riders

Name	Birth Place	Rider Years
1. **Ron Adam**	Saskatoon	1954-60
2. **Barry Aldag**	Gull Lake	1967-72
3. **Roger Aldag**	Gull Lake	1976-92
4. **Mike Anderson**	Regina	1984-95
5. **Paul Anderson**	Saskatoon	1953-59
6. **Ron Atchison**	Central Butte	1952-68
7. **Johnny Babineau**	Saskatoon	1946
8. **Dave Badowich**	Regina	1983-84
9. **Don Bahnuik**	Canora	1966-74
10. **Danny Banda**	Regina	1958-62
11. **Gord Barwell**	Saskatoon	1964-73
12. **Kerry Berryman**	Yorkton	1981-82
13. **Larry Bird**	Big River	1971-78
14. **Gary Brandt**	Regina	1967-77
15. **Rob Bresciani**	Regina	1988-89
16. **Terry Bulych**	Foam Lake	1973-75
17. **Carm Carteri**	Regina	1979-80, 1985
18. **Ken Charlton**	Regina	1941, 1943, 1948-54
19. **Les Charleton**	Regina	1946
20. **Ron Cherkas**	Kamsack	1976-80, 1982, 1985
21. **Dan Clark**	Regina	2009-
22. **William "Bill" Clarke**	Regina	1951-64
23. **Jason Clermont**	Regina	2009-
24. **Bud Curtis**	Saskatoon	1959-60

Name	Birth Place	Rider Years
25. **Lawrence Deck**	Saskatoon	2003-04
26. **Larry DeGraw**	Bracken	1968-70
27. **Duane Dmytryshyn**	Saskatoon	2000
28. **Ken Don**	Saskatoon	1960-62
29. **Hank Dorsch**	Weyburn	1964-71
30. **Larry Dumelie**	Lafleche	1960-67
31. **Rick Dundas**	Regina	1978-79
32. **Ron Dundas**	McKague	1956-60
33. **Ted Dushinski**	Saskatoon	1965-75
34. **Bob Early**	Saskatoon	1948-49
35. **Dan Farthing**	Regina	1991-2001
36. **Adam Faul**	Regina	1946
37. **Brad Fawcett**	Saskatoon	1985
38. **John Fedosoff**	Canora	1958
39. **Gerry Fellner**	Regina	1977-80
40. **Greg Fieger**	Beechy	1980-84
41. **Bill Folk**	Regina	1945-47
42. **Stu Foord**	Regina	2008-
43. **Al Ford**	Regina	1965-76
44. **Jerry Friesen**	Rosthern	1981-86
45. **Tamon George**	Regina	2009-
46. **Chris Getzlaf**	Regina	2008-
47. **George Giokas**	Regina	1947-49
48. **Sully Glasser**	Regina	1946-57
49. **Wilf Godfrey**	Saskatoon	1949

Name	Birth Place	Rider Years
50. **Chuck Gullickson**	Naicam	1963
51. **Nathan Hoffart**	Regina	2005, 2007
52. **John Hoffman**	Regina	1989-92
53. **Jim Hopson**	Regina	1973-76
54. **Gerry Hornett**	Estevan	1979-84
55. **Neal Hughes**	Regina	2004-
56. **Nick Hutchins**	Regina	2009-
57. **Bryan Illerbrun**	Gainsborough	1978-83, 1986-89
58. **Al Johns**	Viscount	1980-87
59. **Dan Johnston**	Regina	1993
60. **Ryan Karhut**	Regina	2007
61. **Doug Killoh**	Qu'Appelle	1953-60
62. **Don King**	Regina	1940-45
63. **Mike Lazecki**	Regina	1990-92
64. **Joel Lipinski**	Regina	2009
65. **Quinn Magnuson**	Saskatoon	1994
66. **Mike Mahoney**	Regina	2005-06
67. **Jim Manz**	Regina	1982-83
68. **Mike Maurer**	Saskatoon	1997-00
69. **Steve Mazurak**	Regina	1973-80
70. **Dane McArthur**	Prince Albert	1991-93
71. **Archie McCord**	Moose Jaw	1971-74
72. **Jack McFarland**	Weyburn	1947
73. **Steve Molnar Jr.**	Saskatoon	1969-78
74. **Steve Molnar Sr.**	Saskatoon	1941

Name	Birth Place	Rider Years
75. **Bob Myers**	Saskatoon	1962-63
76. **Sheldon Napastuk**	North Battleford	1999-02
77. **Brian O'Hara**	Saskatoon	1976-79
78. **Jimmy Partridge**	Outlook	1934-39
79. **Bob Poley**	Saskatoon	1978-84, 1988-92
80. **Brent Pollock**	Regina	1991
81. **Rob Pyne**	Regina	1972-73
82. **Brent Racette**	Prince Albert	1984
83. **Jordan Rempel**	Caronport	2009
84. **Lorne Richardson**	Moose Jaw	1973-76
85. **Dallas Rysavy**	Moose Jaw	1994-96
86. **Scott Schultz**	Moose Jaw	2002-09
87. **Don Seaman**	Wilkie	1969-72
88. **Cliff Shaw**	Bladworth	1966-70
89. **Dave Shaw**	Moose Jaw	1960
90. **Wayne Shaw**	Bladworth	1961-72
91. **Randy Srochenski**	Regina	1994, 1996-2001
92. **Michael Stadnyk**	Regina	2008-09
93. **Kelly Trithart**	Weyburn	1989-93
94. **Lawrie Skolrood**	Saskatoon	1974, 1979-87
95. **Al Urness**	Regina	1926-32
96. **Harold Urness**	Regina	1930-31
97. **Ted Urness**	Regina	1961-70
98. **Jack Urness**	Regina	1958-59
99. **Mark Urness**	Regina	1985-89
100. **Dale West**	Cabri	1962-68

We stopped at 100! Pass along others to: riderbookoflists@hotmail.com

All in the Family
22 Rider Family Ties

Throughout the storied 100 year history of the Riders there were many family connections where siblings, children, and parents shared a bond of participating in the Riders' organization. Here are a few Rider family ties...

*The **Urness** family is at the top of this list, with a remarkable legacy of six Riders.*

1. **Urness:** Albert Urness (1928-1931), younger brother Harold Urness (1930-31); Albert's son Howard Edward "Ted" Urness (C, G, 1961-70), Ted's twin brother Jack Urness (QB, HB, 1958-59); Ted's son Mark Urness (C/G, 1985-89); and Ted's uncle (his mother's brother and Albert Urness' brother-in-law) Fred Goodman (HB, 1929-31).

The remainder of this list is in alphabetical order.

2. **Aldag:** Barry Aldag (G/C, 1967-72) and his younger brother Roger Aldag (C/G, 1976-92).
3. **Anderson:** Paul Anderson (DE, 1953-58), brother Wayne Anderson (HB, 1952), and Paul's son Mike Anderson (C/G, 1984-95).
4. **Boyko:** Bruce Boyko (SB, 1990-96) and his twin brother Allan Boyko (WR, 1991).
5. **James:** Eddie "Dynamite" James (HB, 1928-29, 1931) and his son Gerry James (FB, 1964). Of special note is father and son are both in the Canadian Football Hall of Fame.
6. **Jauch:** Ray Jauch (Asst. Coach 1991-93, and Head Coach, 1994-95) and his son Joey Jauch (SB/WR, 1994-95).
7. **Hackney:** Miller Hackney (player, 1924) and his grandson Campbell Hackney (LB, 1980-82).
8. **Hendrickson:** Craig Hendrickson (OT, 1991-93) and his younger brother Scott Hendrickson (C/G, 1992-97).
9. **Henry:** Lloyd Henry (WR, 1979) and his son Lloyd "Rocky" Henry (WR, 2001-03).
10. **Hungle:** Joe Hungle (G, 1946) and younger brother Tony Hungle (DT, E, 1947-54).

11. **Laird**: Dale Laird, (Equipment manager, 1966-79) and his nephew Rich Laird (ball boy, 1966-68).

12. **Molnar:** Steve Molnar Sr. (player, 1941), and his son Steve Molnar Jr. (FB, 1969-78).

13. **Murphy:** Cal Murphy, (Assistant Coach 1997-99, Head Coach 1999) and his son-in-law Sammy Garza (Assistant Coach, 1998-99).

14. **Pelling:** Bob Pelling, (End, 1947-1953), and his grandson Mike Mahoney, (LB, 2005-06). They both played their first Roughrider game against Montreal.

15. **Preston:** Ken Preston (QB, 1940, 1943, 1946-48, Head Coach 1946-47, and General manager, 1958-78) and his son Rich Preston (ball boy, 1966).

16. **Preston:** Rock Preston (RB, 2001), and his older brother Roell Preston (WR, 2001); playing for the same team in the same year, the duo was nicknamed "Rock and Roll!"

17. **Pyne:** Francis Pyne (OL, 1947), his brother Wayne Pyne (G/T, 1946-53), and Wayne's son Rob Pyne (DB, 1972-73). While attending Tulsa University in Oklahoma, Rob Pyne was coached one year by none other than popular Rider Glenn Dobbs (QB, P, 1951-53).

18. **Rennebohm**: Howard "Tare" Rennebohm (player 1916, 1919-31, equipment manager 1932-57, with some stints in a coaching role) and his son Howard "Tare" Rennebohm Jr. (G, 1946-48).

19. **Scrivener**: Colin Scrivener (DT, 1998-02) and his older brother Glen Scrivener (DT, 1990-91).

20. **Shaw:** Cliff Shaw (LB, 1966-70) and his older brother Wayne Shaw (LB, 1961-72).

21. **Taylor:** Neil "Piffles" Taylor (QB 1914-15, 1919, Executive, 1926-33; President, 1934-36), his brother Sam Taylor (killed 1918 in WW I) who played from 1913-1915, and Piffles' son Sam Taylor was an executive member and president of the club in the 1950s and '60s.

22. **Timmis:** Brian Timmis (RB, 1920-22) and his son Brian Timmis Jr. (HB, 1953).

Know of any other family ties? Contact: riderbookoflists@hotmail.com

Citius, Altius, Fortius! 3 Rider Olympians

Here are three Riders who went *citius, altius, fortius* – the Olympic motto meaning swifter, higher, stronger...

1. **Dan Payne** (Guard/Tackle, 1989, 1993-95)
   Payne was one of 328 athletes representing Canada at the 1988 Seoul Olympics, competing in Men's Super Heavy-weight wrestling in both the Freestyle (6th place) and Greco-Roman (13th place) competitions in the 130 kg division. Canada ended up in 19th place overall against 158 other countries, earning 10 medals (3 gold, 2 silver, 5 bronze.)

2. **George Chiga** (Offensive Lineman, 1934-36)
   Chiga, born in Regina, Saskatchewan, was Canadian heavyweight champion in wrestling (Freestyle) in 1936-37, and went on to represent Canada at the1936 Berlin Summer Olympics. Only 49 countries competed in these Olympic Games, and Chiga was one of 97 Canadian athletes competing. Canada ranked 14th with nine medals (1 gold, 3 silver, 5 bronze). Following service in the Second World War, Chiga settled in the United States. He earned a law degree, practiced law, and became a judge. Following his legal career Chiga became a rancher and developed a popular bloodline of Red Angus cattle. In 2006 Chiga was inducted into the Regina Sports Hall of Fame.

3. **Adam Faul** (Tackle, 1946)
   Another Reginan, Faul played tackle for the Riders at the age of 17 in 1946, although he is most well known for participating in Boxing at the 1948 Summer Olympics in London, England, when he was 19. Faul was one of 118 Canadians at the Games competing against 58 other countries. Canada placed 21st over all, achieving three medals (1 silver and 2 bronze). These were the first Olympic Games to be televised to a home audience. Faul was also the 1947 Light Heavyweight Boxing Champion for Saskatchewan and Canada,, and the 1948 Canadian Heavyweight Boxing Champion. Faul was inducted into the Regina Sports Hall of Fame in 2004.

22 Tall Riders – Over 6'5"

Name	Height	Position	Rider Years
1. **Brad Fawcett**	6'8"	T	1985
2. **Lubo Zizakovic**	6'8"	DT	1995
3. **Joel Bell**	6'7"	T	2009-
4. **Leland Kendall**	6'7"	T	1955-56
5. **Dan Payne**	6'7"	G/T	1989,1993-95
6. **Don Swafford**	6'7"	T	1980, 1982-83
7. **Lyall Woznesensky**	6'7"	DT/DE	1981-82
8. **Dan Goodspeed**	6'6"	OL	2010-
9. **Mike Abou-Mechrek**	6'6"	G/T	2007-08
10. **Nuvraj Bassi**	6'6"	DL	2008
11. **Rob Crifo**	6'6"	SB	1994
12. **Doug Kaufusi**	6'6"	OL	2005
13. **Ronald Flemons**	6'6"	DE	2008
14. **Eddie Freeman**	6'6"	DT	2007
15. **Chad Friehauf**	6'6"	QB	2008
16. **Tim Guy**	6'6"	DE	1977
17. **Cedric Harden**	6'6"	DE	2001
18. **Jean-Francois Morin-Roberge**	6'6"	OL	2008
19. **Neil Plumley**	6'6"	T	1962
20. **Jordan Rempel**	6'6"	T	2009
21. **Milton Robichaux**	6'6"	E	1957
22. **Clifton Washburn**	6'6"	T	2009

36 Not So Tall Riders – Under 5'9"

Name	Height	Position	Rider Years
1. **Bob McKeiver**	5'4"	DB	1958
2. **Richie Hall**	5'6"	DB	1988-91
3. **Dick Imer**	5'6"	HB	1955
4. **Justin Beaver**	5'7"	RB	2009
5. **Curtis Delgardo**	5'7"	RB	1992
6. **Dominique Dorsey**	5'7"	RB	2005-06, 2010-
7. **Weston Dressler**	5'7"	WR	2008-
8. **Tom Ford**	5'7"	HB/FW	1955
9. **Willis Jacox**	5'7"	WR/SB	1987, 1991-92
10. **Peter Shorts**	5'7"	T	1995-96
11. **Craig Yeast**	5'7"	WR	2006
12. **Fred Bailey**	5'8"	WR	1999-2000
13. **Demitris Bendross**	5'8"	WR	2000-02
14. **Errol Brown**	5'8"	S	1993, 1995-97
15. **Davin Bush**	5'8"	DB	2001-06
16. **Hugh Charles**	5'8"	RB	2008-
17. **Jermaine Chatman**	5'8"	DB	2007
18. **Almondo Curry**	5'8"	CB	2006
19. **Darren Davis**	5'8"	RB	2000-01
20. **Michael Elarms**	5'8"	WR	1985-86
21. **Andre Francis**	5'8"	CB	1985
22. **Eric Guliford**	5'8"	WR	1999-2001
23. **Denatay Heard**	5'8"	DB	2008-09

Name	Height	Position	Rider Years
24. **Corey Holmes**	5'8"	RB	2001-05, 2007
25. **James Johnson**	5'8"	DB	2006-08
26. **Doug Kelly**	5'8"	G	1949-51
27. **Ivan MacMillan**	5'8"	PK	1975
28. **Vincent Marshall**	5'8"	WR	2007-08
29. **Ladouphyous McCalla**	5'8"	CB	2000-04
30. **Eric Morris**	5'8"	WR	2009
31. **Rock Preston**	5'8"	RB	2001
32. **Josh Ranek**	5'8"	RB	2007
33. **Carl Roaches**	5'8"	WR	1977
34. **Jeff Treftlin**	5'8"	DB	1988-91
35. **Darrell (Del) Wardien**	5'8"	HB/P	1948-54
36. **Mike Yakymyk**	5'8"	HB	1946-52

7 Multi-Sport (Professional) Riders

Many Riders have well documented multi-sport backgrounds, often playing in various junior and semi-pro hockey and baseball leagues.

Here a few Riders found in the professional ranks of sports other than football...

1. **George Chiga** (Offensive Lineman, 1934-36)
   Chiga, born in Regina, Saskatchewan, was Canadian heavyweight champion in wrestling (Freestyle) in 1936-37, and went on to represent Canada at the 1936 Berlin Summer Olympics. Following service in the Second World War, Chiga settled in the United States. He earned a law degree, practiced law, and became a judge. Following his legal career Chiga became a rancher and developed a popular bloodline of Red Angus cattle. In 2006 Chiga was inducted into the Regina Sports Hall of Fame.
2. **Adam Faul** (Tackle, 1946)
   In 1946 at the relatively young age of 17, Faul played tackle for the Riders, although he is more well known for his participation in the sport of boxing at the 1948 Summer Olympics in London, England. Faul was also the Light Heavyweight Boxing Champion for Saskatchewan and Canada in 1947, and the Canadian Heavyweight Boxing Champion in 1948. Faul was inducted into the Regina Sports Hall of Fame in 2004.
3. **Bill Folk** (Linebacker, 1945-47)
   Folk, born in Regina, went on to play many years in semi-pro and professional hockey. He played for the NHL's Detroit Red Wings in the 1951-52 and 1952-53 seasons, and the Vancouver Canucks in the 1957-58 season.

4. **George Gaiser** (Tackle, 1967)
Gaiser, born in San Antonio, Texas, was drafted by the Buffalo Bills in the 7th round (181st overall) of the 1967 NFL Draft, though ended up in Canada for a brief stint with the Riders. In 1968 Gaiser joined the NFL's Denver Broncos for a single season, playing alongside former Rider Dave Washington (TE, 1963). In 1967 Gaiser made his professional wrestling debut in Houston, Texas, and remained in professional wrestling for approximately the next decade.

5. **Lawrence "Larry" Isbell** (Punter, 1954-58)
While finishing college in the U.S., in 1952 Isbell signed a contract with Major League Baseball's (MLB) Boston Red Sox. Research appears to confirm Isbell played out his baseball career as a catcher in the farm team system for the MLB.

6. **Gerald Edward "Gerry" James** (Fullback, 1964)
James, born in Regina, is the son of former Rider Eddie "Dynamite" James (HB, 1928-29, 1931). Gerry played professional hockey for five seasons (right wing, 1954-60) with the Toronto Maple Leafs of the National Hockey League, and a decade with the CFL's Winnipeg Blue Bombers, all prior to coming home to play with the Riders in 1964. Father and son are both in the Canadian Football Hall of Fame.

7. **Glenn Kulka** (Defensive Tackle, 1995-96)
Kulka played for several other CFL teams before completing his career with the Riders. After football he became a professional wrestler; and was briefly employed by the WWF (World Wrestling Federation). After his wrestling career Kulka spent some time as a sports radio talk show host in Ottawa, and provided on-field commentary for Ottawa Renegade football games.

Double Overtime?
26 Rider Games Ending in a Tie

With or without OT, here are 26 regular season games ending in a tie, including home and away games...

1. **October 17, 2009: Riders 44 – Stampeders 44**
   Game day QB Durant was 35 of 45 for 427 yards and 2 touchdowns. Andy Fantuz caught 10 passes for 149 yards and one touchdown.
2. **July 28, 2000: Riders 52 – Stampeders 52**
   Game day QB Burris was 25 of 45 for 381 yards and five touchdowns.
3. **July 4, 1987: Riders 33 – Argonauts 33**
   Game day actually featured a World Wrestling Federation (WWF) match prior to the game – one of several ticket-selling initiatives of that year. CFL all-stars in 1987 included three Riders: Dave Ridgway (PK), Roger Aldag (C/G), and Bobby Jurasin (DE).
4. **September 14, 1986: Riders 21 – Tiger Cats 21**
   Joe Paopao and Bernard Quarles shared the QB duties that season. Ray Elgaard was the only Rider receiver breaking the 1,000 yard mark in 1986 with 1,003 yards.
5. **July 8, 1984: Riders 27 – Tiger Cats 27**
   Paopao's QB duties were supported by back-up QB Homer Jordan; RB Craig Ellis rushed 141 times for 690 yards on the season, made 91 catches for 871 yards, and returned 42 kickoffs for 1,040 yards.
6. **October 11, 1982: Riders 24 – Tiger Cats 24**
   Joe Adams handled the bulk of the season's QB duties, with John Hufnagel helping out. Slotback Joey Walters had 101 receptions on the season for 1,670 yards.
7. **October 8, 1978: Riders 35 – Alouettes 35**
   Ron Lancaster's last season as the Riders' QB; backed up by Larry Dick. The most prolific pass catcher in this difficult 4-11-1 season was TE Bob Bruer with 491 yards *(Bruer went on to play in the NFL, and he caught Joe Montana's first career touchdown pass).*
8. **September 21, 1975: Riders 28 – Tiger Cats 28**
   The Riders went 10-5-1 with Lancaster as QB. On the season, CB Jim Marshall had seven interceptions, George Reed rushed for 1,454 yds, and Steve Mazurak caught 33 passes for 547 yards and five TDs.

9. **October 17, 1971: Riders 7 – Stampeders 7**
In 1971 the Riders lost the best of three western final series 2-0 to Calgary; Calgary went on to beat Toronto 14-11 to win the Grey Cup, in Vancouver, that was played on artificial turf for the first time.

10. **August 7, 1968: Riders 10 – Eskimos 10**
The Riders were 12-3-1; DB Bob Kosid had eight interceptions on the season, and Gord Barwell led receivers with 40 catches for 783 yards and four touchdowns. The Riders lost the western finals to Calgary. Rider head coach Eagle Keys won the CFL Coach of the Year in 1968.

11. **October 2, 1966: Riders 11 – Blue Bombers 11**
The Riders' leading receiver on this Grey Cup winning season was Hugh Campbell, with 66 receptions for 1,109 yards and 17 TDs.

12. **August 20, 1965: Riders 10 – Lions 10**
George Reed led the CFL in rushing yards with 1,768 on the season, and also earned the CFL's Most Outstanding Player award.

13. **September 14, 1963: Riders 4 – Stampeders 4**
The Riders went 7-7-2 on the season. Defensive Back Dale West had 10 interceptions for 226 yards and one touchdown. The leading receiver was Jack Gotta, with 34 catches for 478 yards and four touchdowns. Rider Punter Martin Fabi set two CFL records in this game that stand to this day: most punts in a regular season game (18), and most punting yards in a regular season game (814).

14. **October 19, 1963: Riders 33 – Stampeders 33**
The Riders lost the western finals to BC. The only Rider named a CFL all-star was Defensive End Garner Ekstran.

15. **August 27, 1962: Riders 7 – Stampeders 7**
QB Bob Ptacek threw for 2,317 yards on the season. Rider Head Coach Steve Owen earned the CFL Coach of the Year award.

16. **October 28, 1961: Riders 17 – Lions 17**
The Riders went 5-10-1 and missed the playoffs under rookie QB Dave Grosz, who took the bulk of the season's snaps in place of injured QB Bob Ptacek. Fullback/Punter Ferdie Burket carried the ball 142 times for 583 yards and three touchdowns.

17. **August 12, 1960: Riders 15 – Stampeders 15**
In this game, QB Bob Ptacek rallied for two touchdowns in the 4th quarter, tossing a 25-yard touchdown pass to Bobby Renn with a minute left. The Riders were 2-12-2 on this difficult season. Bob Ptacek and Don Allard shared the QB duties throughout the season.

18. **October 15, 1960: Riders 14 – Lions 14**
In this game, the Lions rallied in the dying seconds to force the tie. The Riders' reception leader on the season was Bob Renn with 36 catches for 695 yards and eight touchdowns.

19. **September 27, 1958: Riders 11 – Eskimos 11**
Jack Hill led the Riders with 60 receptions for 1,065 yards and 14 TDs on the season, and was the CFL's leading scorer that year.

20. **October 25, 1958: Riders 29 – Stampeders 29**
Cookie Gilchrist rushed 235 times for 1,254 yards and five touchdowns on the season, and QB Frank Tripucka threw for 2,766 yards on the season.

21. **September 30, 1957: Riders 21 – Lions 21**
Harry Lunn returned 28 kickoffs for 699 yards on the season, rushed 54 times for 326 yards and two touchdowns, and caught 11 passes for 163 yards and one touchdown.

22. **September 3, 1954: Riders 12 – Blue Bombers 12**
Rider great Ken Carpenter averaged 37 yards per kickoff return over the season, returning 17 kicks for 630 yards. Carpenter also caught 37 passes on the season for 523 yards and six touchdowns, rushed 110 times for 545 yards and three touchdowns, punted five times for 195 yards, and returned 19 punts for 93 yards.

23. **September 18, 1954: Riders 10 – Blue Bombers 10**
The Riders were 10-4-2 on the season; QB Frank Tripucka threw for 2,003 yards. Bobby Marlow rushed 165 times for 882 yards and four touchdowns.

24. **October 24, 1953: Riders 13 – Stampeders 13**
Head Coach Frank Filchock shared QB duties with Glenn Dobbs and Frank Tripucka during the 1953 season. Mac Speedie was the Riders' leading receiver, catching 57 passes for 817 yards and seven TDs.

25. **October 3, 1936: Riders 6 - Blue Bombers 6**
The Riders, under new player/coach Dean Griffing, beat Winnipeg in the two game total point West Semi Final series and beat Calgary 3-1 in the Western Final. They qualified to go to the Grey Cup, but the league would not let them play their imports (including Griffing) so the team did not challenge for the Grey Cup was an all-eastern affair.

26. **October 26, 1929: Riders 0 - Saskatoon Hilltops 0**
The Riders went 3-1-1 in 1929 and went on to the second (of five) consecutive Grey Cup appearances, losing to Hamilton 14-3.

36 Big Riders – Over 300 lbs.

Rider players over 300 pounds… no more needs to be said…

Name	Weight	Position	Rider Years
1. **Jermese Jones**	337	T	2007
2. **Fred Childress**	331	G/T	2004-06
3. **Dan Clark**	330	OL	2009-
4. **Jean-Francois Morin-Roberge**	325	OL	2008
5. **Amariah Farrow**	325	T	2008
6. **Jordan Rempel**	322	T	2009
7. **Eddie Freeman**	318	DT	2007
8. **Andrew Moore**	315	OL	2001-02
9. **Charles Thomas**	315	T	2003-06
10. **Nick Hutchins**	315	OL	2009-
11. **Chris Best**	315	OL	2007-
12. **Steve Morley**	314	T	2008
13. **Dan Goodspeed**	313	OL	2010-
14. **Donald Heaven**	313	T	2002-04
15. **Doug Kaufusi**	311	OL	2005
16. **Joel Bell**	310	T	2009-
17. **Kelly Bates**	310	G	2010-
18. **Glenn January**	310	T	2008
19. **Jesse Hudson**	310	LB	1975
20. **Jonathan St. Pierre**	310	OL	2009
21. **Bobby Harris**	310	T	2009

Name	Weight	Position	Rider Years
22. **Mike Abou-Mechrek**	305	G/T	2007-08
23. **Rob Lazeo**	305	G	1998-99, 2002-06
24. **Tango McCauley**	305	OL	2003, 2005
25. **Ben Fairbrother**	305	G/T	1997-2000
26. **Andrew Greene**	304	G	1997, 1999-2006
27. **Belton Johnson**	304	T	2007-09
28. **Marc Parenteau**	304	G	2008-
29. **Dan Comiskey**	302	G	1997-2001
30. **Dan Payne**	300	G/T	1989, 1993-95
31. **Clifton Washburn**	300	T	2009
32. **Nate Davis**	300	DT	2001-06
33. **Jimmy Verdon**	300	DT	2008
34. **Val St. Germaine**	300	OL	2007
35. **Jocelyn Frenette**	300	LS	2002-
36. **Jeremy O'Day**	300	C/G	1999-

28 Rider Assistant Coaches Who Became CFL Head Coaches

Here are 28 Rider assistant coaches that were or are currently CFL head coaches...

Name/Years as Rider Assistant Coach	CFL Head Coach
1. **Marcel Bellefeuille**, 2001-05	Hamilton 2008-
2. **Doug Berry**, 2010-	Winnipeg 2006-08
3. **George Brancato**, 1986	Ottawa 1974-84
4. **Steve Buratto**, 1980-82, 1993	Calgary 1984-85, British Columbia 2000-02
5. **Jim Daley**, 1994-95, 2010-	Saskatchewan 1996-98, Winnipeg 2004-05
6. **Larry Donovan**, 1990-91	British Columbia 1987-89
7. **Jim Duncan**, 1965-68	Calgary 1969-73
8. **Jim Eddy**, 1974-76	Saskatchewan 1977-78, Montreal, 1981
9. **Gary Etcheverry**, 2000, 2008-	Toronto 2002
10. **Jim Gilstrap**, 1984-86	Ottawa 1995-96
11. **Steve Goldman**, 1988	Ottawa 1989-91
12. **Jack Gotta**, 1965-67	Ottawa 1970-73, Calgary 1977-83, Saskatchewan 1985-86
13. **Richie Hall**, 1994-2008	Edmonton 2009-
14. **Gary Hoffman**, 1987-92, 1997	Winnipeg 1998
15. **John Hufnagel**, 1987	Calgary 2008-
16. **Ray Jauch**, 1991-93	Edmonton 1970-76, Winnipeg 1978-82, Saskatchewan 1994-95

Name/Years as Rider Assistant Coach	CFL Head Coach
17. **Eagle Keys**, 1964	Edmonton 1959-63, Saskatchewan 1965-70, British Columbia 1971-75
18. **Paul La Police**, 2007-09	Winnipeg 2010-
19. **Ron Lancaster**, 1977-78	Saskatchewan 1979-80, Edmonton 1991-97, Hamilton 1998-02
20. **Joe Moss**, 1977	Toronto 1974, Calgary 1985-1986
21. **Cal Murphy**, 1997-98	British Columbia 1975-76, Winnipeg 1983-86, 1993-96 Saskatchewan 1999
22. **John Payne**, 1971-72	Saskatchewan 1973-76, Hamilton 1978-80, Ottawa 1996
23. **Walt Posadowski**, 1977	Saskatchewan 1978
24. **Bob Price**, 1992-93	Montreal 1996
25. **Bud Riley**, 1973, 1980	Winnipeg 1974-77, Toronto 1978, Hamilton 1982-83, Calgary 1985
26. **Dave Skrein**, 1970	British Columbia 1961-67, Saskatchewan 1971-72
27. **Jim Spavital**, 1968-69	Winnipeg 1970-73
28. **Bob Vespaziani**, 1994, 2000-05	Calgary 1986-87

4 Riders Who Head Coached in the NFL

1. **Frank Filchock - Denver Broncos 1960-61**
   (Rider Quarterback 1953, Head Coach 1953-57)
   Filchock is one the Riders' longest serving head coaches having coached 80 regular season games, and is one of the Riders winningest coaches with a regular season record of 41-35-4. After leaving the Riders following the 1957 season, he coached in Sarnia and was an assistant coach for the Stampders.

   In 1960, he became the first head coach of the Denver Broncos of the newly formed American Football League, under his old Rider GM, Dean Griffing. The Broncos won their first game under Filchock, but the team was never very successful in its ten years before AFL-NFL merger. Filchock left the Broncos after the 1961 season with an overall 7-20-1 regular season record.

2. **Steve Owen - New York Giants 1930-53**
   (Rider Head Coach 1961-62)
   Steve Owen is considered by many to be one of the most influential people in football and is credited with developing the A-formation offense, the umbrella defense, and the two-platoon system. Owen coached for nearly 35 years, including 23 seasons with the New York Giants winning two NFL championships and eight divisional titles.

   Owen played tackle for almost ten years in the NFL prior to coaching full time in the mid 1930s. After leaving the Giants, he was an interim head coach with Toronto and then Calgary, before becoming the Riders' head coach in 1961. The two seasons prior to Owen, the Riders finished well out of the playoffs at 1-15 and 2-12-2. Owen's Riders finished at 5-10-1 in 1961 and 8-7-1 in 1962, making the western playoffs (losing to Calgary). Owen was voted CFL Coach of the Year in 1962, one of only five Rider coaches to have done so. He left the Riders after suffering a heart attack in early 1963, but resumed coaching in the U.S. until his death in 1964. In 1966, he was voted to the Pro Football Hall of Fame.

3. **Mac Speedie - Denver Broncos 1964-66**
   (Rider Wide Receiver 1953-54)
   Speedie was a star receiver with the Cleveland Browns for seven seasons before signing with the Riders in 1953, earning all-star honours in both of his years with the Riders. In 1955, he played for the BC Lions but retired at the end of the season after breaking his leg mid-season.

   In 1960, he became an assistant coach in the newly formed AFL, first with Houston and, before the end of the season, with Denver under his old Rider Head Coach Frank Filchock. Early in the 1964 season, he became Denver's head coach, but the team would struggle throughout the rest of the year and the 1965 season, winning a total of six games in both seasons. Speedie was replaced as head coach two games into the 1966 season, but would be a scout for the Broncos for the next 15 years.

4. **Hugh Campbell - Houston Oilers 1984-85**
   (Rider Wide Receiver 1963-67, 1969)
   After serving as a star receiver for the Riders for much of the 1960s, Campbell served as head coach at Whitworth College in Spokane, Washington, until becoming the head coach for the Edmonton Eskimos in 1977. He took the Eskimos to six straight Grey Cups, winning five consecutive from 1978-1982.

   After a stint as head coach for the USFL's Los Angeles Express, Campbell became head coach of the NFL's Houston Oilers in 1984, reuniting with his old Edmonton quarterback Warren Moon. Campbell's Oilers did not have much success and he was replaced late in the 1984 season. In 1986, he returned to Edmonton as the Eskimos GM, a position he would remain in for 20 years until his retirement in 2006.

13 Rider Dubious Distinctions

1. **Most consecutive Grey Cup losses – 5:** 1928 to 1932.
2. **Most lopsided Grey Cup game – 54-0:** 1923 against Queen's University, the nine touchdowns Queen's scored is also a CFL record.
3. **Highest Shutout Against, Regular Season – 56-0:** July 5, 1985 game in Winnipeg; the Riders also have the second highest shutout against at 55-0 in Edmonton on August 24, 1959.
4. **Most times Shutout, Regular Season – 4***:* this happened in the Riders' 1949 season; the 1954 BC Lions share this distinction.
5. **Most Points Against, Regular Season – 710:** 1991 season; the Riders went 6-12 that season.
6. **Most Interceptions Thrown, Regular Season Game – 8:** the Riders did this twice, in Winnipeg on October 28, 1953, and in Ottawa on September 22, 1974.
7. **Most Interceptions Thrown, Regular Season – 45:** the Riders did this in 1959, so did the 1972 Stampeders and 1990 Ti-Cats.
8. **Most Blocked Kicks, Single Regular Game – 3:** game in Winnipeg on September 13, 1992.
9. **End of Longest Road Losing Streak:** the longest road losing streak in CFL history ended after the Riders lost 40-23 to Montreal on October 9, 1983; the Alouettes had lost 22 away games in a row.
10. **Most Passing Touchdowns in a Single Game – 10:** the Tiger-Cats set this record against the Riders on October 15, 1962 *(needless to say, Hamilton won 67-21).*
11. **Longest Interception Return by a BC Lion – 120 yards:** by Neil Beaumont against the Riders on Oct. 12, 1963 *(BC won 26-6).*
12. **16th Victim - Highest Regular Season Wins:** on November 5, 1989, the Edmonton Eskimos defeated the Riders 49-17 to win their CFL record 16th game of the season. The Riders, however, would have the last laugh and beat the Eskimos in the West Final 32-21, and go on to win the Grey Cup 43-40 against the Ti-Cats.
13. **First Canadian team to lose to a U.S.-based CFL team:** the Sacramento Goldminers beat Saskatchewan 37-26 on July 24, 1993, becoming the first American team to win a regular season CFL game.

The Riders – Denver Broncos Connection

The CFL and the NFL have many connections, though quite possibly no more interesting than those between the Riders and the Denver Broncos...

1. **Dean Griffing** (Rider Centre 1936-41, Head Coach 1936-38, 1940-41, 1943, General Manager 1954-57)
   Broncos' first general manager 1960-61

2. **Frank Filchock** (Rider QB 1953, Head Coach 1953-57)
   Broncos' first head coach 1960-1961

3. **Frank Tripucka** (Rider Quarterback 1953-58, 1963, Head Coach for part of 1959)
   Broncos' first (inaugural roster) quarterback 1960-63
   Broncos' assistant coach 1960-63
   Broncos' Ring of Fame inductee 1986
   Broncos' retired Tripucka's jersey #18

4. **Jim Cason** (Rider Halfback 1953)
   Broncos' first backfield boach 1960

5. **Ken Carpenter** (Rider Running Back 1954-59)
   Broncos' (inaugural roster) wide receiver 1960
   Broncos' assistant coach 1961

6. **George Herring** (Rider Quarterback 1959)
   Broncos' (inaugural roster) punter 1960
   Broncos' quarterback 1961

7. **Jack Hill** (Rider Running Back/Wide Receiver 1957-60)
   Broncos' wide receiver/kicker 1961

8. **Mac Speedie** (Rider Wide Receiver 1953-54)
   Broncos' assistant coach 1960-62
   Broncos' offensive ends coach 1962-64
   Broncos' head coach 1964-66

9. **Cookie Gilchrist** (Rider Halfback/Fullback 1958)
   Broncos' fullback 1965, 1967

10. **Jason Franci** (Rider Wide Receiver 1967-68)
Broncos' wide receiver 1966

11. **Dave Washington** (Rider Tight End 1963)
Broncos' tight end 1968

12. **George Gaiser** (Rider Tackle 1967)
Broncos' guard 1968

13. **John Hufnagel** (Rider Quarterback 1980-83, 1987, Assistant Coach 1987)
Broncos' quarterback 1974-75

14. **Ray Jacobs** (Rider Defensive End 2002)
Broncos' linebacker 1994-95

15. **Matt Dominguez** (Rider Wide Receiver 2003-08)
Broncos' wide receiver 2001-02

16. **Quentin Griffin** (Rider Running Back 2008 - released following final preseason game)
Broncos' running back 2003-05

26 Riders Who Played in the USFL

The United States Football League (USFL) played three seasons between 1983 and 1985, before folding...here are 26 USFL players who played with the Riders...

Name	Position	USFL Team(s)	Rider Years
1. **David Albright**	LB	Memphis Showboats	1986-91
2. **Greg Anderson**	DB	San Antonio Gunslingers	1979
3. **Vickey Ray Anderson**	FB	New Jersey Generals	1979
4. **Jearld Baylis**	DT	New Orleans Breakers/ Portland Breakers	1992-93
5. **Thomas Boyd**	LB	Birmingham Stallions	1982-83
6. **Trent Bryant**	DB	Chicago Blitz Arizona Wranglers	1986-87
7. **Eugene Byrd**	WR	Michigan Panthers	1980
8. **Sammy Greene**	WR	Denver Gold San Antonio Gunslingers	1984
9. **Bobby Hosea**	S/CB	Los Angeles Express Jacksonville Bulls	1980-81
10. **Mike Kelley**	QB	Oakland Invaders Tampa Bay Bandits Memphis Showboats	1986
11. **Mike Loyd**	QB	Oklahoma Outlaws	1982
12. **Mike Matocha**	DE/G	Washington Federals	1980
13. **David McCrary**	DB	Baltimore Stars	1991
14. **Bruce Miller**	CB	New Orleans Breakers/ Portland Breakers	1985

Name	Position	USFL Team(s)	Rider Years
15. **Rick Mohr**	DE	Tampa Bay Bandits Oklahoma Outlaws	1984-85
16. **Ray Odums**	DB	Memphis Showboats	1975-76
17. **Tom Rozantz**	QB	Pittsburgh Maulers Birmingham Stallions, Chicago Blitz	1980
18. **Anthony Parker**	RB	Memphis Showboats	1979
19. **Rodney Parker**	WR	Philadelphia Stars	1978-79
20. **Robert Sparks**	DB/WR	Denver Gold Los Angeles Express	1980
21. **Eddie Ray Walker**	CB	Arizona Wranglers	1985-86, 1988-89
22. **Joey Walters**	WR	Washington Federals Orlando Renegades	1977-82
23. **Bernard West**	LB	Washington Federals Oklahoma Outlaws Orlando Renegades	1981-83
24. **Willie Wilder**	RB	Tampa Bay Bandits	1979
25. **Harold Woods**	DB	Washington Federals	1978
26. **Daric Zeno**	WR	Houston Gamblers	1985-86

Students of the Game? Research Inspired by the Riders

It's not just about the athletics. Here are six research works proving the Riders have an academic, scientific, and analytical appeal too...

1. **"The Saskatchewan Roughriders and the Construction of Identity and Regional Resistance in Saskatchewan, Canada"**
   In this 1999 *Football Studies* journal article (vol. 2, issue 2, pp. 57-76), Dwight H. Zakus of the School of Marketing and Management at Griffith University in Gold Coast, Australia, argues the Riders as an institution are not only a source of community identity, but also demonstrate local/regional resistance to challenges such as Central Canadian political-economic dominance, capitalism in sport (private ownership), and even globalization processes and trends.

2. **"The return of a missed field goal in Canadian football"**
   In this 2001 article in *Chance* (vol. 14, no. 3, pp. 29-33), Keith Willoughby Ph.D., Associate Professor, Department of Finance and Management Science at the University of Saskatchewan Edwards School of Business, develops and applies a mathematical model to the decision to return a missed field goal, or concede the single point. The author used data from the Riders' 1998 regular season (the Riders were 5-13) to examine the relationship between starting field position and scoring. From this, he determined an outcome measure for whether a decision to return or concede was a good one.

3. **"Why Shoot the Gopher? Reading the Politics of a Prairie Icon"**
   In this 2003 journal article in the *American Review of Canadian Studies* (vol. 33, issue 3, pp 391-414), author Alison Calder examines the gopher in prairie popular culture – first as pest and menace, and second as local/regional icon or mascot. It is in the latter capacity of course where Rider mascot Gainer is studied. The two distinct and conflicting representations, she argues, symbolize other prairie conflicts: political dissatisfaction, rural versus urban, cultivation versus conservation, resident versus tourist, indigenous peoples versus settlers, and so on.

4. **"The Migration of African-Americans to the Canadian Football League During the 1950s: An Escape from Racism?"**
In this paper published in 2008 in the *International Journal of the History of Sport* (vol. 25, issue 10, pp. 1374-1397), sports economists Neil Longley, Todd Crosset and Steve Jefferson of the Department of Sport Management at the University of Massachusetts Isenberg School of Management, examine whether African American football players who played in the CFL escaped the racial discrimination that existed in American society and professional sports. Their findings are not very positive. In so doing, the authors also compare the success of a team that employed a high percentage of African-American players (Edmonton) to one that didn't (Saskatchewan) over a ten year period 1951-1960. The results speak for themselves.

5. **"2007 Grey Cup Economic Impact Assessment"**
This analysis from July 2008, undertaken by Tony Fisher of the Canadian Sport Tourism Alliance and Nina Gesa of the City of Toronto, provides an estimate of the economic impact of the 2007 Grey Cup; the first ever between the Saskatchewan Roughriders and the Winnipeg Blue Bombers held in Toronto on the weekend of November 23 to 25th, 2007. The analysis used almost 2,000 spectator surveys and a tourism economic impact assessment model to derive its findings. Total economic activity exceeded $80 million, but of more interest perhaps is that not only did the Riders win on the field (23-19), but spectators from Saskatchewan constituted a larger share of those surveyed than spectators from Manitoba (12.4% to 9.2%). They also spent more per person per day (almost $3,000 compared to $2,758), including more on accommodation, food/beverage and Grey Cup merchandise.

6. **"What the Saskatchewan Roughriders Have Taught Me about Pharmacy"**
In this 2010 article published in *The Canadian Journal of Hospital Pharmacy* (vol. 63, no. 2, March–April 2010, p. 184), author Jason Howorko examines the parallels between the Rider Nation experience and the pharmacy profession. Of course his primary inspiration appears to be the shared ecstasy and agony of the final plays of the 2009 season. Howorko relates the parallels through the following constructs: Dream Big; Vision and Leadership; Teamwork; Communication; Accountability; Little Plays Make a Difference; Attention to Detail; and Pride, Passion and Inspiration. The author ponders if the dawn of a "Pharmacist Nation" is on the horizon.

The Results Are In! 10 Winningest Rider Head Coaches

Here it is, the winningest Rider head coaches that have coached 20 or more regular season and playoff games.

Head Coach Years as Coach	Regular Season Record	Playoff Record	Overall Percentage
1. **Al Ritchie** 1930-32, 1935, 1942	.947 (18-1)	.643 (9-5)	**.818**
2. **Kent Austin** 2007	.667 (12-6)	1.00 (3-0)	**.714**
3. **Fred Ritter** 1910-13	.625 (10-6)	1.00 (4-0)	**.700**
4. **Eagle Keys** 1965-70	.724 (68-25-3)	.529 (9-8)	**.695**
5. **John Payne** 1973-76	.633 (40-23-1)	.500 (4-4)	**.618**
6. **Ken Miller** 2008-09	.625 (22-13-1)	.333 (1-2)	**.603**
7. **Dave Skrien** 1971-72	.547 (17-14-1)	.500 (3-3)	**.539**
8. **Frank Filchock** 1953-57	.538 (41-35-4)	.409 (4-6-1)	**.522**
9. **Bob Shaw** 1963-64	.531 (16-14-2)	.429 (3-4)	**.513**
10. **Don Matthews** 1991-93	.522 (24-22)	.000 (0-2)	**.500**

Data compiled by the authors up to the end of the 2009 season. Ties awarded a half-win in determining percentages. Playoff records include Grey Cups. Prior to 1967, the West Semi Final was a two game total point series and prior to 1972 the West Final was a best of three series.

18 Rider Grey Cup Firsts, Lasts & Records

They may not have won many, but the Riders have been involved in a number of Grey Cup records and milestones. Here are 18 of them...

1. **Most lopsided score – 54-0 (1923)**
   Loss to Queen's University at Toronto.
2. **Most consecutive Grey Cup berths (not appearances) – 7 (1926-32)**
   The Riders actually qualified for the Grey Cup in both 1926 and 1927, but due to the month or more delay from the end of the Riders season to the Cup game (because of the lateness of the Eastern playoffs), they did not challenge for the Grey Cup. The Edmonton Eskimos hold the record for most consecutive Grey Cup appearances at 6 (1977 to 1982).
3. **Most consecutive losses – 5 (1928-1932)**
4. **First radio play-by-play broadcast – 1928**
   The 16th Grey Cup in Hamilton was the first to feature radio play by play; the Riders lost 30-0 to the Hamilton Tigers.
5. **First forward pass thrown in Grey Cup game – 1929**
   This was the first year the forward pass was permitted in Grey Cup competition and it was the Riders' Jersey Jack Campbell who threw the first one. It was the 17th Grey Cup in Hamilton and the Riders lost 14-3.
6. **First Grey Cup Rematch – 1928 & 1929**
   The Riders met the Hamilton Tigers in back-to-back Grey Cups in 1928 and 1929, losing both times.
7. **The West's first Grey Cup touchdown – 1930**
   Edmonton didn't do it in 1921 or 1922, Winnipeg didn't do it in 1925, and the Riders didn't do it in 1928 or 1929, but in the 1930 Grey Cup in Toronto the Riders finally did it for the West – on a rushing play. Interestingly, after being allowed the forward pass the year before, the Riders were not allowed to use it in 1930 because of a Canadian Rugby Union rule change.

8. **First Grey Cup game played outside Ontario – 1931**
The 19th Grey Cup in 1931 was held in Montreal; the Riders lost 22-0 to the Montreal Winged Wheelers (also called Montreal AAA).

9. **First Western Official in a Grey Cup Game – 1931**
No wonder the West Division fared so bad in early Grey Cups! The 19th Grey Cup in 1931, the first Grey Cup played outside Ontario (in Montreal), was also the first time one of the officials refereeing the Grey Cup was from the West. The Riders lost 22-0 to Montreal. The official was Howie Milne, a Rider player from 1920-28 and head coach from 1926-28. Milne is also a member of the Saskatchewan Sports Hall of Fame.

10. **First Grey Cup televised in colour – 1966**
The 54th Grey Cup, in 1966, in Vancouver was the Riders first Grey Cup victory, a 29-14 win over Ottawa, and it was televised in colour on CBC.

11. **First (and last) Grey Cup game played at Montreal's Autostade – 1969**
The 57th grey Cup in 1969 was in Montreal's Autostade; the Riders lost 29-11 to Ottawa. The stadium was demolished in 1977 (see 9 Stadiums the Riders Won't Play in Again).

12. **Last Grey Cup played in December – 1972**
The 60th Grey Cup in 1972 was in Hamilton and was the last one played in December; the Riders lost 13-10 to Hamilton on the final play of the game.

13. **Highest total points scored – 83**
The thrilling 1989 Grey Cup in Toronto, a 43-40 Rider win over Hamilton, was the highest total points ever scored in a Cup game.

14. **First Grey Cup played in Toronto's Skydome (now Rogers Centre) – 1989**
The 77th Grey Cup in 1989, a 43-40 Rider win over Hamilton.

15. **First head coach to win a Grey Cup for the same team for which he won the championship as a quarterback – Kent Austin (1989 & 2007)**
Both times in Toronto: the 77th Grey Cup in 1989, as quarterback, and the 95th Grey Cup in 2007, as head coach.

16. **Last Grey Cup game broadcast free over the air – 2007**
The 95th Grey Cup in 2007, in Toronto, where the Riders won 23-19 over Winnipeg was the last Grey Cup game broadcast nationally on conventional TV by the CBC. In 2008, The Sports Network (TSN) became the exclusive broadcaster of all CFL games - regular and post season.

17. **First Grey Cup game between 'Western' rivals – 2007**
The Grey Cup was exclusively an all-eastern affair from 1909-21, and 1944 was the last time two eastern teams competed against each other for the Cup. The 95th Grey Cup in 2007, in Toronto, where the Riders beat the Bombers 23-19, was the first time two western rivals competed against each other (*come on, we all know Winnipeg rightfully belongs in the West...*).

18. **First Grey Cup to feature live posted blogs and updates on national internet media – 2009**
The 97th Grey Cup in 2009, in Calgary, was the first to feature live play by play on posted blogs in national internet media; the Riders lost 28-27 to Montreal on the final play of the game.

Bronks, Elks, & Altomahs Rider Opponents of the Past

Some teams (and team names) that played against the Riders but didn't last nearly as long...

1. **Calgary Tigers, Canucks, and Fiftieth Battalion**
   Calgary's first football team was named the Tigers until 1915, and then the Canucks until 1919. In 1923, when football resumed in the city the team was called the Fiftieth Battalion (the battalion provided the team with support), and played until 1924. In 1928 the Tigers resurfaced.

2. **Calgary Altomahs and Calgary Bronks**
   In 1931, the Calgary Altomahs (also called the Altomah-Tigers) were formed and were renamed the Calgary Bronks in 1935, until the 1940s when once again football was suspended in the city, this time due to WWII. The Riders beat the Bronks in the Western Finals in 1936, and lost to them in the semi-finals in 1938. In 1945, the team's name was officially changed to the Stampeders and its first game as such was against the Riders.

3. **Edmonton Elks**
   It's not real clear why, but for some reason the Edmonton Eskimos changed their name to the Elks in 1922 and, after beating the Riders in the playoffs, made it all the way to the Grey Cup (like Eskimos did the year before). Edmonton lost, like they did the year before, and would not make it back to the Grey Cup until 1952 (as the Eskimos again).

4. **Montreal Winged Wheelers**
   Football in Québec goes back to the 1860s, and the Montreal Winged Wheelers played as early as 1881 and continued under that name until 1935. They were the first eastern team not from Ontario to play in, and win, the Grey Cup, beating the Roughriders 22-0 at Montreal's Molson Stadium in 1931.

5. **Sarnia Imperials**
The Imperials made it to the Grey Cup in 1933, 1934 and 1936, twice under dubious circumstances. In 1933, it was because they hosted the game and the West finalist had to play the East finalist to get to the Grey Cup. In 1936, the league ruled five Riders ineligible, and so the West champion Riders chose not to play for the Cup and the winner of the East final was declared Grey Cup champion. In 1934, however, Sarnia finished first in the East and beat the Riders 20-12 in the Grey Cup.

6. **Winnipeg Winnipegs**
Winnipeg's early football scene featured a number of teams, often with strange names such as the Victorias, Rowing Club, the Johnnies (also called St. John's), and the Winnipeg Tammany Tigers. In 1930, all of the city's teams were merged into one team – and apparently the best name they could come up with was the Winnipegs or 'Pegs. The team beat the Riders in the western finals in 1933 but had to play Toronto to get to the Grey Cup (see the Sarnia Imperials above). They lost, but in 1935 the Winnipegs became the first western team in ten attempts to win the Grey Cup, and a year later the team became known as the Blue Bombers.

7. **Miami Manatees**
Okay, the Riders didn't actually play a game against the Manatees, but they might have in 1996 if the move of Las Vegas' much-troubled CFL franchise had gone ahead. The plans fell through after Baltimore moved to Montreal and the remaining U.S. based CFL teams disbanded after the 1995 season. The Riders did play against the Sacramento Gold Miners, Baltimore Stallions, Shreveport Pirates, San Antonio Texans, Memphis Mad Dogs, and Las Vegas Posse.

Placeholders
27 Riders for Whom Places Are Named

So, there are lists for trophies named after Riders, Riders in Halls of Fame, and Riders who hold records...here are 27 Riders with places of various sorts named after them...

1. **Neil J. "Piffles" Taylor**
   Quarterback (1914-15-1919) Executive/President (1926-1936)
   - Taylor Field; Piffles Taylor Way (street), and 1910 Piffles Taylor Way (Rider Football Club street address); all in Regina, SK
2. **Alvin Horace (Al) Ritchie**
   Manager (1921-24), Head Coach (1929-32, 1935, 1942)
   - Al Ritchie Memorial Centre (indoor arena), Ritchie Crescent and Core/Al Ritchie subdivision (neighbourhood), Regina, SK
3. **Ron Lancaster**
   Quarterback (1963-1978), Head Coach (1979-1980)
   - Lancaster Place (street), Regina, SK
4. **Glenn Dobbs**
   Quarterback/Punter/HC (1951-53)
   - Glenn Dobbs Drive, University of Tulsa, Tulsa, Oklahoma
5. **Mario DeMarco**
   Guard (1953-56)
   - DeMarco Drive and DeMarco 2nd Avenue Park, Regina, SK
6. **Mel Becket**
   Centre (1953-56)
   - Beckett (sic) Place (street), Regina, SK
7. **George Reed**
   Running Back (1963-75)
   - Reed Place (street), Regina, SK
8. **S. D. "Stack" Tibbits**
   President (1949)
   - Tibbitts Road and Tibbitts Park, Regina, SK

9. **Gord Staseson**
President (1979-1982)
- Gordon Staseson Boulevard, Regina, SK

10. **Ron Atchison**
Defensive Tackle (1952-68)
- Atchison Crescent, Regina, SK, Atchison Field, Saskatoon, SK (Hilltops practice field) and Atchison Lake, SK

11. **Howie Milne**
Player (1920-1928), Head Coach (1926-28)
- Milne Street and Sherwood/Milne Park, Regina, SK

12. **Ken Charlton**
Running Back (1941, 1943, 1948-54)
- Charlton Place (street), Regina, SK

13. **Johnny Garuik**
Offensive Line (1930-43)
- Garuik Park and Playground, and Garuik Crescent, Regina, SK

14. **Gordon Barber**
Player/Executive (1929-33)
- Barber Street, Regina, SK

15. **Brian Timmis**
Player/Executive (1929-33)
- Brian Timmis Stadium adjacent to Ivor Wynne Stadium, Hamilton, Ontario; and Brian Timmis Parkette at the corner of Balsam and Cannon, across from Brian Timmis Stadium's parking lot.

16. **Clair Warner**
Player (1919, 1924-33), President (1945), General Manager (1946-49, 1951-52)
- Warner Bay, Regina, SK

17. **Clarence "Toar" Springstein**
Tackle (1939-41, 1946, 1949-52)
- Springstein Avenue, Regina, SK

18. **Wally Dempsey**
Linebacker (1965-69, 1972)
- Dempsey Avenue, Regina, SK

19. **Adam Faul**
Tackle (1946)
- Faul Bay, Regina, SK

20. **Richard "Dick" Rendek**
Director/President (1982-84)
- Rendek Crescent and Rendek Avenue, Regina, SK

21. **Bruce Cowie**
President (1976-78)
- Cowie Road, Regina, SK

22. **Jack Hartman**
Quarterback (1950)
- Jack Hartman Drive, Kansas State University, Manhattan, Kansas

23. **Robert Leith "Dinny" Hanbidge**
Tackle (1910-14)
- Hanbidge Crescent, Regina, SK; Hanbidge Building, Kerrobert, SK

24. **Steve Sarkisian**
Quarterback (1997-99)
- "Sarcade"; ok, it may be cyberspace, but it's a space and its inspired by Steve Sarkisian and features online arcade games at www.coachsark.com

25. **Galen Wahlmeier**
Centre/Long Snapper/Linebacker (1957, 1959-63, 1965-67)
- Wahlmeier Drive, Estevan, SK

26. **Charles Leibel**
Player (1951)
- Leibel Field, Regina, SK

27. **The Saskatchewan Roughriders**
1910-present
- The Green Mile, Regina, SK (Albert Street, north from Regina Avenue to Piffles Taylor Way – Taylor Field/Mosaic Stadium

Know of any other places named after Riders? Send them along to: riderbookoflists@hotmail.com

17 Interesting Individual Rider Firsts

Here is a list of individual achievements where a Rider was first in some way, whether before, during or after their time with the team...

1. **Fred Brown** (Outside Wing 1929-30)
   Brown's 55 yard **interception return for a touchdown** was the first ever scored in Canadian football. It was against the Calgary Tigers in the 1929 Western Final, which became the first team to use the forward pass in Canadian football. In 1930, Fred Brown also scored the **first Rider Grey Cup touchdown** (and the first by a Western team) when he recovered an onside kick in the end zone against Balmy Beach; the Riders lost 11-6.
2. **Robert Ellis "Stonewall" Jackson** (Middle Wing/HB 1930)
   Although official sources note Herb Trawick and Virgil Wagner of the 1946 Montreal Alouettes as the **first African-American players** in the CFL, Stonewall Jackson played middle wing/halfback for at least one game with the 1930 Regina Roughriders (and is in the team picture and mentioned in newspaper articles from that year).
3. **Jersey Jack Campbell** (Quarterback 1929-35)
   Campbell was the **first to throw a forward pass in a Grey Cup game**; 1929 was the first time the forward pass was permitted in Grey Cup competition. It fell incomplete, but the rules at the time still allowed the ball to be playable and fortunately the Riders recovered. The Riders lost the game 14-3 to the Hamilton Tigers.
4. **William A. R. (Bill) Orban** (Halfback 1941-42)
   Born in Regina, some have called Orban Canada's pioneer of physical fitness. Orban is credited with being the **first Canadian accepted to the University of California's physical education program**; a member of the **first graduating class in the physical education program at McGill University**; and **the first scientist to participate in developing Canada's national fitness test**. While working for the federal government in the 1950s, Orban developed the 5BX Plan (five basic exercises) for Canadian Air Force pilots. Orban was also **the first Canadian to earn a doctorate degree (Ph.D.) in Exercise Physiology**. He was inducted in the Saskatchewan Sports Hall of Fame in 2003.

5. **Frank Tripucka** (Quarterback 1953-59, 1963)
Tripucka played with the 1960 Denver Broncos, the team's first season along with the formation of the American Football League (AFL). He became their first starting quarterback and has the distinction of having thrown the **first touchdown pass in AFL history** (to Al Carmichael on September 9, 1960 at Boston). The AFL merged with the National Football League in 1970. Tripucka played with the team for four seasons, and was the **first U.S. pro quarterback to throw for 3,000 yards in a season**. Interestingly, Tripucka is one of a handful of former Riders who were instrumental in the Broncos' inaugural season, including Dean Griffing, (Rider player, coach and GM) who became the Broncos' first GM, and Frank Filchock (Rider QB and head coach) who was the team's first head coach, and Ken Carpenter (Rider running back and head coach) who also played with Denver in 1960.

6. **Ed McQuarters** (Defensive Tackle 1966-74)
McQuarters was the **first African-American high school state wrestling champ** from Oklahoma, and when he wrestled Joe James in 1963, it was the first time two African-Americans had competed against each other in the annual "Bedlam" series of contests between the University of Oklahoma and Oklahoma State University.

7. **Carlton Chester "Cookie" Gilchrist** (Halfback/FB 1958)
Gilchrist was a bruising fullback and linebacker, who was so good the Cleveland Browns tried to sign him straight out of high school. It took a special ruling from NFL Commissioner Bert Bell to allow the 19 year old to join the Browns in 1954. When he didn't make the first cut-down in the preseason, Gilchrist went north, playing rugby with the Sarnia Imperials before signing with the Hamilton Tiger-Cats in 1956. He helped Hamilton win the 1957 Grey Cup, scoring two touchdowns. He played for the Riders in 1958 before joining the Buffalo Bills of the American Football League that formed in 1960. He became **the AFL's first 1,000 yard rusher** and reached the AFL All-Star game four times. His final all-star appearance was his most famous: Gilchrist led a successful anti-segregation protest to have a football game moved from New Orleans to Houston.

8. **Jim Worden** (Tight End 1964-69)
Worden holds the distinction of scoring the **Saskatchewan Roughriders' first touchdown in the club's first Grey Cup victory** in 1966, after catching a nine-yard pass from Ron Lancaster.

9. **Bob Bruer** (Tight End 1977-78)
After his time with the Riders, Bruer went on to play in the NFL with the San Francisco 49ers. He **caught the first touchdown pass of NFL Hall of Fame Quarterback Joe Montana** on November 18, 1979, while playing against the Denver Broncos.

10. **Joey Walters** (Wide Receiver 1977-82)
Star receiver Walters left the Riders for the Washington Federals of the USFL in 1983 and became the **first trade in the USFL**, when he was traded from Washington to Michigan for LB Mel Land and WR Frank McCrimmon (and 4th pick in 1984 Draft), on February 20, 1983. During a large part of Walters' time with the Washington Federals (before they folded after the 1983 and 1984 seasons), the team's head coach was none other than former Rider assistant coach (1991-93), and later head coach (1994-95), Ray Jauch.

11. **Jeff Bentrim** (Quarterback 1987-90)
Bentrim was the **first winner of the Harlon Hill Trophy** in 1986. The trophy is awarded to the United States NCAA Division II Football player of the year.

12. **Glenn Dobbs** (Quarterback/Punter 1951-53, Head Coach 1952) **and Martin Ruby** (Tackle 1951-57)
Dobbs and Ruby both played in the 1944 Cotton Bowl Classic between the University of Texas and Randolph Field, which featured a few firsts. It was the **first (and only) time a military team** played in the game (Randolph Field – an airbase in San Antonio). It was the **first tied Cotton Bowl** game (7-7); there have since been two other tied games (in 1947 and 1948). Both Dobbs and Ruby played for Randolph Field and both were named outstanding players of the game. For Ruby, he became the **first (and only) player to be named outstanding player for two different Cotton Bowl Classic teams** – Randolph Field in 1944 and Texas A & M in 1942.

13. **Clyde "Lee" Grosscup** (Quarterback 1963)
Lee Grosscup joined a group of Rider QBs in 1963, though unfortunately for him it was the beginning of the Ron Lancaster era. Before joining the Riders, Grosscup played three seasons with the NFL's New York Jets. Grosscup went on to have a long TV sports broadcasting career in the U.S. He was the **first "Voice of the Gold Miners"** colour analyst for the short-lived Sacramento Gold Miners, as part of the failed CFL expansion into the U.S.

14. **Roy Shivers** (General Manager 1999-2006)
and Danny Barrett (Head Coach 2000-06)
Roy Shivers was the **first African-American general manager in professional football** when he joined the short-lived U.S. expansion franchise in Birmingham that folded after one season in 1995. Upon becoming the Riders' General Manager, and when he hired Danny Barrett as Rider head Coach in 2000, the two became **the first African-American GM and head coach in professional sports**.

15. **Kent Austin** (Quarterback 1987-93, Head Coach 2007)
In winning the Riders' third Grey Cup, Austin became the first head coach to win a Grey Cup for the same team for which he won the championship as a quarterback.

16. **Ken Preston** (Quarterback 1940, 1943, 1946-48, Head Coach 1946-47, GM 1958-78)
As the General Manager of the Riders, in 1961 Preston established for the Riders the **first deferred salary savings plan** for players in the CFL.

17. **James "Jimmy" Partridge** (player 1934-39)
Born in 1913 in Outlook, Saskatchewan, Partridge enlisted in the Canadian military on November 24, 1939, and became a pilot with the No. 424 Squadron of the Royal Canadian Air Force, participating with allied forces fighting against Nazi Germany.

    In 1944 King George VI approved awarding Flight Lieutenant James Alfred "Jimmy" Partridge the Distinguished Flying Cross ". . . in recognition of gallantry displayed in flying operations against the enemy." Partridge is **the first (and quite possibly the only for all-time) Rider to receive the Distinguished Flying Cross**. He piloted 28 dangerous sorties over parts of Europe in the spring and summer of 1944. The medal was sent to Partridge by registered mail on April 20, 1949.

Riders by the Numbers – 1 to 100

A fan favourite...naming Riders in order by jersey number...

Jersey Number/Name	Position	Rider Years
1. **Willie Cullpepper**	Wide Receiver	1993
2. **Eddie Ray Walker**	Defensive Back	1985-86, 1988-89
3. **Gerry McGrath**	Punter	1985-86
4. **Darian Durant**	Quarterback	2006 -
5. **Kent Austin**	Quarterback	1987-93
6. **Dexter Dawson**	Wide Receiver	1998
7. **Weston Dressler**	Wide Receiver	2008 -
8. **Homer Jordan**	Quarterback	1983-85
9. **Sully Glasser**	Fullback/QB	1946-57
10. **Luca Congi**	Placekicker	2006 -
11. **Darnell Edwards**	Defensive Back	2002-06
12. **Dale West**	Defensive Back	1962-68
13. **Gainer the Gopher**	Mascot	1977
14. **Bob Ptacek**	Quarterback/LB	1960-65
15. **Nealon Greene**	Quarterback	2003-05
16. **Brian O'Hara**	Slotback	1976-79
17. **Dick McQuaid**	Halfback	1946-47
18. **Jeff Fairholm**	Slotback	1988-93
19. **Emanuel Tolbert**	Wide Receiver	1980-82
20. **Tony Hungle**	Defensive Tackle/End	1947-54
21. **Tommy Reamon**	Halfback	1977
22. **Stu Foord**	Running Back	2008-
23. **Ron Lancaster**	Quarterback	1963-78

Jersey Number/Name	Position	Rider Years
24. **Bob Kosid**	Defensive Back	1964-72
25. **Steve Dennis**	Cornerback	1977-84
26. **Larry Dumelie**	Defensive Back	1960-67
27. **Ted Dushinski**	Defensive Back	1965-75
28. **Matt Hammer**	Defensive Back	1999-00
29. **Eddie Davis**	Halfback	2001-09
30. **Bruce Bennett**	Defensive Back	1966-72
31. **Hugh Campbell**	Wide Receiver	1963-67, 1969
32. **Mike Saunders**	Running Back	1992-94, 1997-99
33. **Dwight Edwards**	Wide Receiver	1980-83
34. **George Reed**	Running Back	1963-75
35. **Rick Walters**	Running Back/SB	1994-98
36. **Dave Ridgway**	Placekicker	1982-95
37. **Roger Goree**	Linebacker	1975-80
38. **Dave Badowich**	Punter	1983-84
39. **Dave Albright**	Linebacker	1986-91
40. **Mel Becket**	Centre	1953-56
41. **Ron Atchison**	Defensive Tackle	1952-68
42. **Galen Wahlmeier**	Linebacker	1957-62, 1965-68
43. **Ted Urness**	Centre/Guard	1961-70
44. **Roger Aldag**	Centre/Guard	1976-92
45. **Glenn Dobbs**	Quarterback/Punter	1951-53
46. **Armand Boglin**	Linebacker	2001-02
47. **Kelly Trithart**	Linebacker	1989-93
48. **Anton McKenzie**	Linebacker	2006-08

Jersey Number/Name	Position	Rider Years
49. **Mike Mahoney**	Linebacker	2005-06
50. **Mike Cassidy**	Offensive Tackle/DE	1948-55
51. **Cliff Shaw**	Linebacker	1966-70
52. **Barry Aldag**	Guard/Centre	1967-72
53. **Jack Abendschan**	Placekicker/Guard	1965-75
54. **Garner Ekstran**	Defensive End	1961-67
55. **Mario DeMarco**	Guard	1953-56
56. **Ray Syrnyk**	Guard	1954-56
57. **Gary Brandt**	Guard	1967-77
58. **Ken Reed**	Defensive End/LB	1965-70
59. **Craig Hendrickson**	Offensive Tackle	1991-93
60. **Gene Makowsky**	Guard	1995-
61. **Ed McQuarters**	Defensive Tackle	1966-74
62. **Reg Whitehouse**	Offensive Tackle/G	1952-66
63. **Scott Hendrickson**	Centre/Guard	1992-97
64. **Shawn Gifford**	Offensive Lineman	2001-02
65. **Moe Levesque**	Defensive Tackle	1966
66. **Mike Anderson**	Centre/Guard	1984-95
67. **Clyde Brock**	Offensive Tackle	1964-75
68. **Len Legault**	Defensive Tackle	1957-65
69. **Russ Haines**	Guard/Tackle	1958-60
70. **Steve Mazurak**	Wide Receiver	1973-80
71. **Bobby Jurasin**	Defensive End	1986-97
72. **Jim Worden**	Tight End	1964-69
73. **Gordon Sturtridge**	Defensive End	1953-56

Jersey Number/Name	Position	Rider Years
74. **Jack Gotta**	Wide Receiver	1960-64
75. **Bill Manchuk**	Linebacker	1971-80
76. **Tyson St. James**	Defensive End/LB	2000-02
77. **Lawrie Skolrood**	Tight End/OT	1974,1979-87
78. **Vince Goldsmith**	Defensive End/LB	1981-83, 1988-90
79. **Martin Fabi**	Punter/Tight End	1962-65
80. **Frank Filchock**	Quarterback	1953
81. **Ray Elgaard**	Slotback	1983-96
82. **Jason Clermont**	Slotback	2009-
83. **Andy Fantuz**	Slotback	2006-
84. **Elijah Thurmon**	Wide Receiver	2004-05
85. **Karsten Bailey**	Wide Receiver	2004-05
86. **Nathan Hoffart**	Slotback	2005-07
87. **Joey Jauch**	Slotback	1994-95
88. **Matt Dominguez**	Wide Receiver	2003-08
89. **Chris Getzlaf**	Wide Receiver	2008-
90. **Del Wardien**	Halfback/Punter	1948-54
91. **Ferdie Burket**	Fullback/Punter	1959-62
92. **Bobby Marlow**	Fullback/Linebacker	1953-60
93. **Jack Urness**	Quarterback/Halfback	1958-59
94. **Henry Newby**	Linebacker	1997
95. **Luc Mullinder**	Defensive Lineman	2004-
96. **Scott Schultz**	Defensive Tackle	2001-09
97. **Brooks Findlay**	Linebacker	1993-96, 2001
98. **Bobby Flippin**	Halfback	1954
99. **Chance McCarty**	Defensive End	2000
100. **Gainer the Gopher**	Mascot	*2010 season*

References & Contributing Sources

Websites

The authors thank the following organizations, associations, companies and individuals with websites containing factual and/or contextual information that contributed to the development or verification of some lists. Any errors or omissions in this list are unintentional.

Access 7 Community Channel
Air Force Association of Canada
AFL Internet Network
Athletes in Action Canada
BC Lions
Board Game Geek
620 CKRM
Calgary Stampeders
canada.com
The Canadian Encyclopedia
Canadian Football Hall of Fame
Canadian Football League
The Canadian Football League Alumni Association (CFLAA)
Canadian Football League Players Association (CFLPA)
Canadian Olympic Committee
canoe.ca
The Carillon
CBC News
cflapedia.com
CJAY 92
City of Regina
City of Edmonton
City of Toronto
clubsask.com
The Comedy Network
conigliofamily.com
Crown Investments Corporation of Saskatchewan
CTV News
Dal Richards
Denver Broncos
Edmonton Eskimos
Encyclopedia of Saskatchewan
expolounge.blogspot.com
Facebook
fanbase.com
Faster Gun
Five Stones Films
The Florida Times-Union
Friends of Canadian Broadcasting
gendisasters.com
GeorgiaTrend
Getting Fit Again

Google, Google Books, Google News Canada, Google Scholar

Governor General of Canada

greenzonefootball.com

Hamilton Tiger-Cats

Harlan Hill Trophy

Heisman Trophy

hockeyDB.com

Holy Cross University

InterMat

Internet Movie Database

Jason Plumb

Jeff McQuarrie

Jersey City

LA84 Foundation

Lawrence Journal-World

Legends of the Palouse

Lieutenant Governor of Saskatchewan

The London Gazette (UK)

Lytton Financial

McGill University

memorialstadium.org

The Milwaukee Journal

mmbolding.com

Montreal Alouettes

The Montreal Gazette

mykaussie.com

National Capital Football Coaches Association

National Film Board of Canada

National Football League

The NFL Internet Network

The National Football Foundation
and College Hall of Fame Inc.

NBC.com

New York Giants

The New York Times

North American Association of Sports Economists

The Ottawa Citizen

Our Sports Central

Packers.com

Paperback Swap

Pro Football Hall of Fame

Pro-Football-Reference.com

Puget Sound Radio

Professional Football Researchers Association

Regina Leader Post

Regina Sports Hall of Fame

Rick Mercer Report

Riderville.com

River City Sports

rodpedersen.blogspot.com

ROI Resources

The Sacramento Bee

Sark

Saskatchewan Arts Alliance

Saskatchewan Ministry of Education

Saskatchewan News Index

Saskatchewan Roughriders Pep Band

Saskatchewan Sports Hall of Fame

Saskatoon Star Phoenix

SaskTel

Schizophrenia Society of Saskatchewan

SLAM! Sports

The Spokesman-Review

sportsnet.ca

the-kramerfamily.com

Toronto Argonauts

Tourism Saskatchewan

truthandrumours.net

TSN.ca

Twitter

University of Regina

University of Saskatchewan

University of Tulsa

University of Utah

USFL.info

The Vancouver Sun

Vinyl Records

The War Amps

Western Canada Baseball

Wide Mouth Mason

Wikipedia

Winnipeg Blue Bombers

Wittenberg University

Wrestling Lutte Canada

YouTube

Books & Publications

Argan, William P. (2002). *Regina, the First 100 Years*. Regina, SK: Leader Post Carrier Foundation.

Argan, William P. with Pam Cowan. (1995). Cornerstones: *An Artists History of the City of Regina*. Regina, SK: Leader Post Carrier Foundation.

Calder, Bob & Andrews, Gary. (1984). *Rider Pride: The Story of Canada's Best-Loved Football Team*. Saskatoon, SK: Western Producer Prairie Books.

Calder, B., Slaseson, G., Folk, J., Hughes, B., Vanstone, R., Davis D. and Marce, Dan (eds.). (2009). *Saskatchewan Roughriders First 100 Years*. Regina, SK: Leader-Post Carrier Foundation.

Kelly, Graham. (1999). *The Grey Cup: A History*. Red Deer, AB: Johnson Gorman Publishers.

Kelly, Graham. (2001). *Green Grit – An Illustrated History of the Saskatchewan Roughriders*. Toronto, ON: HarperCollins Canada.

Maxymuk, John. (2007). *Strong Arm Tactics: A History and Statistical Analysis of the Professional Quarterback*, Jefferson, NC: McFarland.

Mein, Lillian and Mein, Stewart (eds.). (1992). *Regina, The Street Where You Live: Origins of Regina Street Names*. Regina, SK: Regina Public Library

Phillips, Curt. (2010). *The Canadian Football Rushers Compendium*. Regina, SK: published by the author.

Phillips, Curt. (2003). *The Professional Football Head Coach Register*. Regina, SK: published by the author.

Phillips, Curt. (1997). *Saskatchewan Roughrider Player Reference 1960-1996*. Regina, SK: published by the author.

Porter, David L. (1995). *Biographical Dictionary of American Sports, 6th Volume*. Santa Barbara, CA: Greenwood Press.

Powers, Ned. (2006). *The Hilltops: A Canadian Junior Football Legacy*, Saskatoon, SK: Saskatoon Hilltop Football Club.

Ryczek, William J. (2009). *Crash of the Titans: The Early Years of the New York Jets and the AFL*. Jefferson, NC: McFarland.

Saskatchewan Roughriders Football Club. (2009). *Saskatchewan Roughriders 2009 Media Guide*. Regina, SK: Saskatchewan Roughriders Football Club.

Thiele, Stephen. (1997). *Heroes of the Game: A History of the Grey Cup*. Norval, ON: Moulin Publishing.

The War Amps, and Chadderton, H Clifford. (2006). *Jeff Nicklin – Hero of the Gridiron and The Battlefield* (screenplay). H. Clifford Chadderton Productions.

Yuen, Edward. (2002). *92Years of Roughrider Football*. Regina, SK: published by the author.

Zimmer, Larry. (2004). *Denver Broncos: Colorful Tales of the Orange and Blue*: New York: Globe Pequot Press.